BX 4705 .␣␣␣ ‖‖‖‖‖‖‖‖‖‖‖‖‖‖‖‖‖‖‖‖‖‖‖

Matus, Thomas.   S0-AIT-324

Nazarena

NAZARENA

An American Anchoress

by
Thomas Matus

HOLY SPIRIT LIBRARY
CABRINI COLLEGE, RADNOR, PA.

Paulist Press
New York/ Mahwah, N.J.

BX
4705
.C78366
M38
1998

XX 385 42759

The Publisher gratefully acknowledges use of the following: Extracts from the letters of Nazarena. Copyright by The Camaldolese Benedictine Nuns of the Monastery Sant'Antonio Abate in Rome. Extract from poem #998 taken from *The Complete Poems of Emily Dickinson,* edited by Thomas H. Johnson. Copyright 1960. Reprinted by permission of Little, Brown and Company. Extract from poem #998 also reprinted by permission of the publishers and the Trustees of Amherst College from *The Poems of Emily Dickinson,* Thomas H. Johnson, ed., Cambridge, Mass.: The Belknap Press of Harvard University Press, Copyright 1951, 1955, 1979, 1983 by the President and Fellows of Harvard College. Used with permission.

Photos on cover: Sister Nazarena's cell, at Sant'Antonio, as she left it at death, February 7, 1990. Julia in Camaldolese habit, at Sant'Antonio, Rome, circa 1938. The Crotta family, circa 1905, shortly after they arrived from Italy. In the back row, left to right, are Caroline, Lawrence and Paul; Louis, their father, has Jane in his lap; Rose is in the center, and Maria is seated on the right. The photo does not show Elizabeth and Julia, born in 1906 and 1907, respectively, in the United States. All photos are property of The Camaldolese Benedictine Nuns of the Monastery of Sant'Antonio Abate in Rome. Used with permission.

Digital processing of photographic material by Duane Palyka.

Copyright © 1998 by Thomas Matus

All rights reserved. No part of this book may be reproduced or transmitted in any form or by any means, electronic or mechanical, including photocopying, recording or by any information storage and retrieval system without permission in writing from the Publisher.

Library of Congress Cataloging-in-Publication Data

Matus, Thomas.
   Nazarena : an American anchoress / by Thomas Matus.
     p. cm.
   Includes bibliographical references.
   ISBN 0-8091-3792-5 (alk. paper)
    1. Crotta, Julia, 1907–1990.   2. Camaldolese—Italy—Rome—Biography.
I. Title.
BX4705.C78366M38   1998
271'.97—dc21
[B]
                                          98-14691
                                             CIP

Cover design by Kathy McKeen
Interior design by Joseph E. Petta
Typeset in 11/13 Berkeley Oldstyle

Published by Paulist Press
997 Macarthur Boulevard
Mahwah, New Jersey 07430

Printed and bound in the
United States of America

Contents

Julia seated in front of parents' home:
Connecticut, ca. 1935

PROLOGUE
The Call

The tall, young woman knelt motionless in the dark. In her long, lithe violinist's fingers she held a rosary, but she was reciting no prayers. No sanctuary lamp lit the empty tabernacle and the bare altar, for it was the night between Good Friday and Holy Saturday, when churches are silent and believers relive the grief of the disciples after their Master's crucifixion.

A man's soft voice broke the silence, calling her name: "Julia," he said.

She looked over her shoulder to see if someone had entered the chapel, although the voice was clearly not coming from behind her. She was still alone. The gentle voice repeated insistently, "Julia!" It sounded very near.

She did not move. The darkness parted slowly before her eyes and a bright column of light assumed the shape of a man, stripped and wounded. He said, "Julia, I'm all alone—come with me to the desert! I'll never leave you!"

Julia felt no fear. She knew who the man was. Fixing her gaze on his eyes she saw love, greater than all the love she had known in her life. Without words she gave him her consent. Then the darkness and silence of the chapel embraced her, and she wept for joy.

An indeterminate time passed, and the Dominican sisters began to arrive for their morning vigil service. Julia wiped her eyes and took a seat in the back of the chapel, as the sisters began the *Tenebrae* prayers.

The Holy Week of 1934, at Albertus Magnus College in Connecticut, was Julia Crotta's first retreat. She had entered the college a year before, transferring from Yale. She was twenty-six years old. Although Julia was a good Catholic, in no way was she a candidate for visions or mystical raptures. Her parents were Italian; they were well-to-do farmers, simple, hard-working, and affectionate. She was their youngest daughter, born in Connecticut; two of her sisters were born in New York, but her two brothers and the two elder sisters were born in Italy. She had studied piano, violin, and composition at the Yale School of Music, had briefly been a chorus girl in New York City, and now was in her junior year at Albertus.

Julia had boyfriends, but something in her strong, willful nature both attracted and repelled them. She was inclined to think she ought to remain single, although not as a nun. But the man with the wounds in his hands, who spoke to her during the night between Good Friday and Holy Saturday, promised her something she had never dreamed of, something more than a marriage. He was the Man of Sorrows, but the love he gave her in that happy night was pure joy and peace for her soul. She could never love anyone else as she loved him.

It took Julia eleven years to find her way to the desert. Every priest she told of the vision judged it an illusion, a dream, a psychotic symptom. In 1937 a Jesuit in New York advised her to go to Rome. After five years there as a Carmelite nun she walked out of the convent into a city at war, because she heard the voice again: "Julia, I called you to the desert. What are you doing in a convent?"

She thought "the desert" meant the wilderness of Judah, but she found it only a few blocks away, on the Aventine Hill overlooking the ruins of imperial Rome: the monastery of Saint Antony of Egypt. While priests and Carmelites alike regarded her call to the desert as pathological, the nuns of

Sant'Antonio on the Aventine welcomed her into their midst as an anchoress, a "recluse," in accordance with the eremitical spirit of their order. They were Camaldolese, daughters of Saint Benedict and of an anchorite who lived in the year 1000, Romuald of Ravenna. Julia entered the monastery in 1945, and from then on was known as Sister Nazarena.

My own life as a monk was from the first entwined with that of the American anchoress. I learned about Nazarena from *Time* magazine. An article in the April 12, 1962, issue described her life at the monastery in Rome, with a photograph of her in a white habit. I already felt drawn to live as a monk, perhaps at New Camaldoli Hermitage in Big Sur, and so I said a prayer to the Holy Spirit: "Inspire her to pray for my vocation." I felt I might realize my calling among the Camaldolese Benedictines if she were praying for me, even though she did not know me. Two months later I entered the novitiate at Big Sur.

But New Camaldoli was not to be my permanent home. After five years there, I was sent to continue my studies at the Benedictine college in Rome, and on earning my degree I decided to stay in Italy, at the Monastery of Camaldoli in the Tuscan Apennines.

I often thought about Sister Nazarena. I wondered whether she might leave her cell one day to found a hermitage for women in the United States. But I never felt curious enough to ask if I might speak with her or write her a letter. It was enough for me to know she was there.

Sister Nazarena died on February 7, 1990. I was in California at the time, with my brothers in Big Sur. In March I returned to Rome and went to pay a visit to the Camaldolese nuns. The abbess asked if I would like to see her cell. I was pleasantly surprised and said yes.

She took me up to the large workroom on the third floor. One of the two doors at the end of the room led to the abbess's office, the other to Nazarena's reclusion. The abbess unlocked the door, and we entered a narrow vestibule, where the priest used to sit while hearing her confession and where the nuns would leave food, other necessities, and the materials for her manual labor. A second door had a metal grate covered with a piece of burlap; the anchoress could be heard without being seen. The abbess unlocked the second door. The room was dark; she threw open a large window, and soft spring sunlight flooded the room. It was clean and bare; the only furnishings were three large cabinets, a bookcase, two low stools—all of unvarnished wood—and a bamboo armchair. The chair had been brought to her room on the evening of her death.

Mother Abbess said, "You may stay here as long as you like," and she left.

A succession of strong feelings began to flow through my soul. The first sensation was that of being welcomed by a relative or a close friend. I felt perfectly at ease. At the same time, I realized that this was a place like the cave of the burning bush, and like Moses I took off my shoes.

At the first thought of addressing a word to the departed anchoress I almost heard something—a "voice" both strong and gentle telling me to address my prayers to God alone. And then came an invitation to enter into the same quiet, spiritual space where Nazarena prayed. My mind became very still, and I knelt for several minutes on the floor. Then I sat on one of the stools. From time to time a thought came to me. At a certain point I sensed that Sister Nazarena was happy with my dialogue with Buddhist and Hindu monks. I also thought of the liturgical music I was writing for the community and of the repugnance I felt for this task, and the answer came: Finish the work and then forget it.

An hour passed, and I began to examine the room in detail. To the right of the inner door was a large box, a yard high and wide and two yards long. On the lid was a broad cross, about an inch thick. At night Nazarena would throw a rough quilt over the box and sleep there for three or four hours. Hanging in the cabinet to the left was her robe; the fabric was of rough wool, like sackcloth, except for the veil, a broad piece of cotton muslin.

I was sitting on the smaller of two stools, the one she used occasionally as a footrest (she always went barefoot, in winter as in summer). There was no table; another small box served the purpose. A book in English lay there, a scholarly commentary on the Psalms. I read the page it was open to, wondering if this were the last page she meditated on, the morning of the day she died. A bookcase along the end wall was full of a variety of volumes, mostly the sort of "spiritual reading" you expect to find in a nun's room. But there were also a few books in English, including a translation of documents of the Second Vatican Council. Above the bookcase was a wooden cross, an image of the Blessed Virgin, and a calendar.

Another cabinet contained a variety of tools—pliers, scissors, and so forth—that Nazarena used for her work, the weaving of ornate crosses out of palm fronds for the Vatican Holy Week services. There were also her tools of penance: a cummerbund of horsehair, a belt of chains, a wooden cross with nails that penetrated through to the side worn next to the skin. These instruments offended my rational concept of monastic balance and discretion—even the older Italian monks who had trained me at Big Sur and in Rome had warned me against playing this sort of ascetical game. But again a voice that made no sound told me that Nazarena's purpose was not to punish the body but to keep the mind centered and grounded; the penitential exercises served as a remedy for the fantasies and illusions that constantly plague hermits and anchorites. On the wall the nuns had tacked a few photographs of the anchoress and a copy of the *Time* magazine article that had been decisive for my own monastic choice.

The *Angelus* bell interrupted my meditations. I had been in Nazarena's cell for three hours. I went and thanked the abbess and returned to the monastery of Saint Gregory on the Coelian hill, a ten-minute walk from the nuns' convent.

I visited the anchoress's cell a couple of times more, and again I felt the mysterious silence that made me temporarily unaware of the city noises that came in through the open window. Soon after her death a few hasty publications made Sister Nazarena known in Italy and France, but the Camaldolese nuns on the Aventine found them unsatisfactory and asked me to write a book about her. In 1992 I began translating the several hundred letters the American anchoress had written to her Sisters, which they keep in neat boxes in the monastery archives. To help me understand the prophecy hidden in her life, I asked her confessor and my former superior, don Anselmo Giabbani, to tell me the story of their friendship. His recollections, together with those of the abbess and the nuns, were the thread on which I have strung the words and deeds of Sister Nazarena.[1]

PART ONE
A Desert Journey

1. Julia's Story

A thousand years ago, in the days when Romuald of Ravenna, father of the Camaldolese Benedictines, was briefly abbot of Sant'Apollinare in Classe and Adalbert of Prague was martyred by Prussian tribes in northern Poland, a family by the name of Crotta already possessed rich farmlands in the valley of the Po.[1] Italy's great river flowed from Piedmont through Lombardy into a vast and swampy delta south of Venice, which included the Vales of Comacchio above Ravenna. The Crotta family spread out along the Po; you find records of them in Bérgamo to the north, in Piacenza and Parma to the south, and all the way east to Venice. Even today you can see the name Crotta inscribed on a tomb at the entrance to the former Camaldolese monastery of San Michele, now Venice's cemetery.

Julia's branch of the family settled in the province of Piacenza, near a town called Ferriere; they were there some time before 1714. One hundred and fifty years later Julia's father, Luigi, was born, and at the age of twenty-three he married a girl from a nearby village, Maria Ramponi.

Those were hard times in the province of Piacenza, and since Maria had relatives who were farming the land in New England, Luigi left his family and emigrated to New York. The year was 1898;[2] after five years of hard work he brought his wife and their four children to the United States. After they arrived, a family photograph was taken. Luigi was now called Louis, and although he and Maria still conversed in their Lombardy dialect, they were committed to raising their children as Americans. They never looked back to Italy with nostalgia.[3]

The Crottas were an unusually close-knit family. Maria was a watchful mother but not possessive, and she trained her children to be free and responsible persons. Louis was a quiet man, seldom angry and never harsh; he had a strength of character that enabled him to correct and discipline his children without severity—his example was enough, along with a few gentle words of approval or disapproval.

Louis and Maria had two more daughters, Jane and Elizabeth, in New York; the last of their seven children, Julia, was born in Glastonbury, Connecticut, on October 15, 1907. Maria's cousins, the Scaglias, had been in northern Connecticut for a good number of years. With other Italian families in the area, they formed a fruit and orchard farming cooperative; the rural setting and the supportive community were a much better environment than New York for raising a large family. Louis's skills and the family's hard work soon won them a reputation for the best peaches grown in Glastonbury.

The Crottas were good Catholics; the women of the family attended mass every Sunday, the men less frequently. Mamma Maria sent the children to catechism as a matter of course, and all took First Communion and Confirmation. Three miles from their farm was the small parish church, where Julia was baptized on December 1, 1907; the Scaglias stood as her godparents.[4]

Julia was a bright child and remembered many events of her infancy. One memory, however, was reawakened by her mother in a setting of intense and painful emotions. In the second week of November 1937, a few days before she took ship for Rome, Julia visited her family for the last time.[5] Julia's elder sisters, Rosa and Caroline, sat with their babies asleep in their laps; the two had given birth the preceding summer, within a few days of each other.

Mamma Maria said, "Look how quiet your nieces are, Julia. How different you were, always restless. I could never leave you in the crib, or you would cry, and I'd have to take you out. But I always kept an eye on you, because you would crawl off to another room. One day I was in the kitchen, and I put you on the floor of the pantry. You were making a great noise with the pot lids. I turn around, and what do I see? You come walking toward me with a lid in your hand! Julia, you were only seven months old!"

Rosa interrupted her mother. "Mamma, you must be mistaken. Babies can't even stand up at seven months, much less walk!"

"I am not mistaken," Mamma replied emphatically. "This is a true story!"

Julia's sisters treasure other stories about her childhood. At the age of four, Julia was playing outdoors near the home of family friends when a sudden storm broke, with hurricane gusts so strong a man was lifted off his feet and tossed about in the air. Lightning struck the house and it partly collapsed. Julia, thrown to the ground, lay lifeless in what seemed to be a pool of blood. The baby-sitter ran to tell Mamma Maria, who fainted for fright. Louis sent for a doctor and ran to the neighbors' house, but when he got there he saw his little daughter standing on her feet, wet and dirty but stubbornly alive. Louis gathered her up in his arms and took her to her mother.[6]

One day as four-year-old Julia was playing with her sisters and the neighbors' children, a strange thought came to her mind: "My sisters and these other girls will get married and have babies, but I shall never be married." She began to think, "I can't get married, because I am going to do something unusual." Julia had no idea what this "something unusual" meant, but she felt sure it would be made clear to her one day.[7]

This lively child, the darling of her middle-aged parents, developed a streak of unbending willfulness; usually obedient, she would refuse with stony silence a request or an order she judged wrong.[8] At the end of her life, the anchoress wrote to her mother abbess: "Severity, scolding, punishment had no effect on me. I always felt the deep need—and I feel it more strongly now than ever—to act with total freedom, out of love. Love alone enabled me to overcome difficulties and to do things that required great sacrifice."

Julia's insatiable appetite became a family joke. Hers was an appetite for both quantity and quality of food, but she was especially addicted to chocolate. Mamma Maria was an excellent cook and the best pastry chef in the zone. Her specialty was chocolate cake, with a smooth frosting that she spread thickly over the top and sides. While preparing the meal she would leave the cake in the pantry, and later she would discover that the extra frosting around the sides of the cake had been wiped clean. "Julia did it again!" the family would say, and laugh.

Once for Mother's Day they gave Maria a box of fancy chocolates. Mamma Maria took one and gave the box to Julia, saying, "You can have one, and then take the box to my bedroom." Julia ate two chocolates, and then a third, and left the box on her mother's dressing table. A few days later a friend of her mother's came, bringing her young son. Maria told Julia, "Go fetch a chocolate for the little boy." Julia stood there, blushing. She was forced to admit that the box was empty, because she had eaten them all.

The only moderation Julia practiced was on great family feasts, when her mother and Rosa would prepare a variety of desserts. Julia would go into the pantry, without touching anything; she would make a mental note of the desserts she liked most, and then at table would take very little of the main course, to save room for double helpings of dessert.[9]

By the Light of the Star of Hope

In 1916 Louis and Maria bought their own dairy and tobacco farm near Ellington, Connecticut. Julia attended public elementary school there; the family's parish church was located some distance away in the town of Rockville, where Julia was confirmed.[10]

She asked herself, "What name should I choose for Confirmation?" Like a flash the answer came: "Choose Hope!" Although she was not sure it was an appropriate name for a girl, that was her choice. In a letter to her confessor, Nazarena wrote, "Jesus illumined the sky of my soul with the splendor of the star of hope. Without the light of that star, how could I ever have found the way to my vocation?"[11] "I bless God for an iron-clad hope—how many years I have had to struggle with various and violent temptations against hope!"[12]

One day, Julia went to confession. Instead of the usual two or three sins, she told the priest, "I committed robbery." The priest realized that this was the voice of a little girl, and after a moment of silence he asked her, "Did you rob a bank?" "No," Julia said. "Did you rob the grocery store?" "No," she said again. So the priest recited a list of all the things a nine-year-old might steal, and the answer was always, "Not that." Finally the priest said, "If you do not tell me what you stole, your confession is not complete, and I cannot give you absolution." So with a very faint voice, Julia admitted, "I took some cookies from the pantry." "But that's not robbery!" the priest exclaimed. "Yes, Father, but I didn't know what sin it was, so 'robbery' seemed the best thing to say."[13]

Her sister Elizabeth remembers her at that time: "She was very devout, much more particular about church attendance than anyone else in the family."[14] But Sister Nazarena, looking back on her childhood, did not see herself as a particularly religious girl. Confession was an occasional formality, for which she prepared by memorizing textbook sins and saying them quickly in the confessional. The priest was usually satisfied and asked her no questions.

Julia was a serious girl and took her religious duties seriously, but for her they were precisely that: duties. While she took little pleasure in games and parties—these were also "social duties" to be observed—she did not enjoy long liturgical functions either. The Crottas were not any more devout than their neighbors. The rosary was not a family prayer, except during the month of May, when every evening after supper Mamma Maria made the girls kneel down for rosary and our Lady's litany. Julia endured it as her greatest penance.[15] In church, when the sermon was long or the ceremonies were particularly elaborate, she would start squirming in the pew and ask, "How much longer?"

And yet, when she happened to be near the church and nobody was watching, she would go inside and enjoy the darkness and silence. There she would kneel down, without saying any particular prayers, and think, "Jesus is in here!"[16]

By 1921 only the two youngest girls, Elizabeth and Julia, remained with their parents; the others had married and purchased their own homes. Louis sold the dairy and moved to a seven-acre truck farm on the outskirts of Rockville, where Julia enrolled in the public high school.[17]

Julia was not only strong-willed; she grew tall and threw herself into sports, especially basketball. But she channeled her energies of body and mind mostly into music. She had begun to study piano at an early age, and by the time she entered high school, she was giving solo recitals for her family and friends. At school assemblies the principal would call on her to accompany the national anthem or "America the Beautiful," which she did with great pleasure. She strove for the highest marks and would laugh with delight when her name appeared high on the honors' list. Yet she was more than an achiever—she took real pleasure in studying and would devour books with the same avidity with which she devoured food.[18]

"She had some boyfriends from time to time," said one of Julia's nieces, "but nothing serious ever seemed to develop."[19] She admitted that a certain trait of severity in her personality made them shy away. "If a boy started to flirt with me, I turned my back on him. Once one of my girlfriends told me a boy had asked her to ask me if I would go to a party with him, since he was too shy to ask me personally. I refused. Even some of the girls were afraid of me."[20]

By their good example, Louis and Maria Crotta transmitted a strong work ethic to their children. Every summer from high school through college, Julia had a job. Elizabeth found work as a waitress at a summer resort in the Catskills, and in the summer of 1925 Julia joined her there.[21]

In June 1926 Julia graduated from high school and immediately asked her parents to let her go to New York—Rosa had moved there with her husband and their baby.[22] In New York Julia continued to practice the piano and signed up for dance lessons at a school for chorus girls. After a couple of months she realized there was no way she could keep a job as a chorus girl and continue her music at the same time. Above all, she wanted to start violin lessons.

Mamma and Papà worried about Julia, alone in New York, studying dance and mixing with theater people. But Julia was nearly six feet tall, and she had a will of iron. She never missed mass once, even though she had to get up very early on Sunday to attend church, since her dance classes and chorus rehearsals were seven days a week. When she had a little free time, she attended Benediction in the evening. She later wrote, "Jesus began to draw me to himself, and I think that if I had spoken with a priest, he would probably have made me enter a religious order. But that was not God's will for me, then."[23]

Julia returned to her parents' home and in the fall of 1926 entered the Hartford Conservatory, where she studied violin, piano, and musical theory. Summers she went with Elizabeth to work in the Catskills. In 1929 she sought admission to the Yale School of Music. She began a full course in violin—two weekly lessons with the renowned virtuoso Hugo Kortschak—and studied composition with David Stanley Smith and Richard Donovan. A modestly gifted young violinist by the name of Benjamin Kubelski was among Kortschak's students; he later became famous as the comedian Jack Benny.

By June 1932 she had her diploma and planned to continue another two years for the academic degree. But in early September, as she walked across the campus to the music building, a strong voice flashed like lightning through her mind: "Quit Yale and prepare to transfer to Albertus Magnus Women's College!" Albertus was a Catholic school with an excellent reputation for its liberal arts course.

When she reached the School of Music, she asked the registrar to give her a transcript of her grades, since she was quitting Yale. As Julia walked out, the dean of the school, Professor Smith, called out to her, "Miss Crotta, you have talent!" She pretended not to hear and continued walking toward the door. He ran after her, saying again, "You have talent!" He reminded her that at the end of her third year one of her pieces, a Fugue in C for piano, had been performed at the year-end recital.[24] Normally only compositions by students in the advanced Free Composition seminar were performed in public; it was a rare exception when works of third-year students were included on the program. But Professor Smith was unable to make her turn back.

Changing schools did not change Julia's lifestyle. Although there were Dominican sisters among her professors at Albertus, Julia did not consider joining their order. She continued to be just a good Sunday Catholic, fulfilling her religious duties and avoiding social activities so that she could channel all her time and energy into study and music.

The following year Julia's niece, Mary Rita—ten years her junior—joined her there, and they became good friends. "At college Julia was very good to me, and she really helped me to find my way in the new environment," reminisced Mary Rita. "However, our interests were quite different—she was working on languages and literature, while my interests were in science. Julia was well liked, quiet, and had some very good friends, some of whom still inquire about her. She was very religious and never missed church. She was very determined and firm—an 'all or nothing' sort of person. At one time, Julia tried her hand at writing a movie script, which she submitted to some Hollywood studio, without results. Her screenplay was entitled *How Dare You*."[25] The script was discarded by the studio, and Julia kept no copy.

The Blessed Night

One day in March 1934, Julia went to the registrar's office, and the Sister asked if she had ever made a retreat. She said no. "Would you like to join us for the Holy Week retreat?" the Sister suggested. Again, Julia said no. But the nun insisted, and she accepted the invitation.[26]

Julia entered into the rhythm of ceremonies, sermons, and evening devotions. Before the liturgical reforms, the Latin services of Holy Week were celebrated in mid-morning; the afternoon "Way of the Cross" assumed the character of a vernacular liturgy. The retreatants took turns watching in adoration at the sepulchre or altar of reposition, where the Eucharist consecrated at Thursday's Mass was kept for Communion on Good Friday. After the Passion service, the altar was stripped of its linens, and the tabernacle remained empty.

The bare altar attracted Julia. On Friday evening the chapel was like the dark and quiet parish church she loved as a child. Perhaps a Sister was in the sacristy for a short while, making sure everything was ready for the Resurrection liturgy of Saturday morning. Then she was alone.

"Jesus is in here," little Julia used to say, as she sat in a corner of the empty parish church. And now, in the deserted convent chapel, she renewed this act of faith. If a wave of sleepiness came over her, it promptly yielded to her will to remain vigilant and focused on the unveiled crucifix.

She heard a voice calling her name, "Julia!" She turned and

looked behind her, but she already knew the voice did not come from without. "Julia!" it said, again and again.

She saw a man who stood weeping before her. He stretched out his wounded hands. He called her to the desert and promised her his abiding presence. She answered him with an unspoken yes.

Silence returned, and she saw the man no more. Julia was weeping, but hers were tears of joy. She had known a love she had never imagined could find room in a human heart. Soon the sound of a wooden clapper summoned the Sisters to choir. She wiped her tears and listened to the Psalms and the Lamentations of Jeremiah.

In those days the *Praeconium Paschale,* the deacon's great song before the Easter candle, was sung on Holy Saturday. Its words, which Julia followed in her missal, were paradoxical, because on that morning of the last day of March, the deacon was singing of night, *O nox!* Paradox was intrinsic to the liturgical text, because it coupled the noun *culpa,* "fault, guilt," with the adjective *felix,* "happy." "O happy fault, O truly necessary sin of Adam, which deserved so great a Savior!" The meaning of Julia's vision became clear in this liturgy of Christ's Resurrection. He who had called her was the Man of Sorrows, but now she felt the joy of the Risen Lord. She had known his love and heard his promise: "I shall never leave you." From henceforth, the night of her call would abide in her memory as a *nox beatissima,* "a most blessed night."

The change in her was deep; the vision, she would say later, "instantly transformed my entire existence."[27] And yet no one noticed any outward sign of this new life. Julia kept her feet firmly planted on the ground of concrete tasks and duties, even when her eyes and heart were drawn to heaven. She returned to college and to the normal round of classes and preparations for final examinations. Her junior year ended with the usual high marks; she saw her name on the honors' list, and with her niece Mary Rita she left to join Elizabeth for the summer job in the Catskills.

Julia had not yet spoken to anyone about her vision, except once, in the confessional, to a priest. He told her, "It was all your imagination!"[28] She decided that, from then on, she would never mention it again. Julia had the good sense to realize that the vision of Jesus might have been a once-in-a-lifetime experience, but even though she was not expecting other visions, many strange and beautiful dreams came to her that spring, and she remembered them still at the end of her life.

"I see myself as a grown woman, wandering in a circular corridor without doors. Suddenly I find a way out, and a marvelous scene opens up before me: woods and meadows and a lake, in the face of which the natural beauties of this world seem lifeless. I have no words to describe them, but I think they must be the trees and waters of 'the new earth and the new heavens' about which the Bible speaks.[29] At this, I become very small, like a little girl of three or four years. Could it mean that the tall and proud woman I am has at last been made humble, and I have become a little one? As I gaze on the beauties of the scene, I hear a sound to my left. I turn and see Jesus walking toward me; behind him is a great multitude of little girls and boys. When he reaches me, he stoops down and takes me up into his arms. He continues on his way, holding me close to his heart, with the multitude of children following in his steps."

Nazarena inserts her interpretation into the dream itself: Her question, whether the "proud woman" she considered herself to be was now becoming a "little one" is a theological interpretation, a reflection on the meaning of her passage from a religion of duty and willpower to an intimate relationship with a gracious Creator, who stoops down from on high to lift up the creature and carry her in the ways of gratuitous grace.

Another dream bears a similar reading. "I see myself in a church. I wait kneeling before the altar, arrayed in bridal finery, with a veil of unusual size and beauty. Then I behold the face of Jesus radiant with unspeakable glory. Every time I think of this vision, I remember the transfiguration on Mount Thabor—Oh, what will it be to see his visage by the light of glory, to gaze face to face on the figure of Beauty itself, shining forth in all its majesty! But as I kneel before the altar I am unable to focus on the features of the radiant Jesus. I feel that he is gazing on me with great love and that he desires to unite me to himself. And this is what I desire too. I think: He desires to be one with me, and I with him— why then has the union not taken place? Then another thought pierces me like an arrow: it cannot take place, because there is an obstacle.... Then all vanishes."

Years later, when the dream came back to her, she doubted it was from God. "The dream cannot have been true," she told herself. "The dimensions and the magnificence of the bridal veil are exaggerated; not even an empress would wear a veil like that." But the voice within reassured her that the dream was indeed true, and that the unusual size and beauty of the veil were a symbol of the virtues with which the soul must be adorned before it can be raised to the union with Jesus that is its destiny. And another time, as she was writing an inventory of her faults, it came to her more clearly than ever: The veil is the virtue of humility, which covers all faults. Humility alone will remove the obstacles to union.[30]

Nazarena narrated a third dream that came following the vision: "I see monks seated around a table. Other persons are present, but they are out of my line of sight. The monks ask one another what could possibly be God's will for me. After much deliberation, they decide that it is the will of God that I enter a religious order. They say, 'After much time she will found in the Church a state of life more austere than any the Church has ever approved.'"[31] This dream seems to be the contrary of the others. Julia wants to hear voices of approval from the official church, and she wants her entry into an existing order to be the preparation for a future role as "foundress." The transformation has begun, but the Spirit still needs to work on Julia's pride, before she can truly become a little one.

The Search for the Desert

At first Julia could not fathom the meaning of Jesus' words, "Come with me to the desert." She often rehearsed the moment of her vision and the dialogue with Jesus, his promise never to leave her, in spite of the sufferings she would have to endure. She prayed for his grace, that she might faithfully follow the call to the desert.[32] Later, speaking with confessors and counselors, she would put forth various and contradictory hypotheses about where the "desert" was to be found. But for the moment, her choice was to get on with her life, finish her degree, and ground herself in a regular rhythm of prayer and work.

Without taking counsel with anyone, Julia began to practice various "mortifications." This change in her natural habits was a gradual process, which began with early rising, daily Communion, and fasting. The winter of 1934–1935 in New England was exceptionally cold. Julia, who was always susceptible to chills, began to leave her window open in the evening, as she knelt in her sleeveless, low-cut nightgown on the floor by the bed. There she would remain, trembling, for an hour and more. During the day she would dread the bedtime penance, but she continued it with her usual determination.

For a brief period she placed shards of broken crockery in the middle of her bed, but this penance lasted only a few days.

She took lunch in the campus dining hall and ate what was served, but she sought to mortify her palate by renouncing salt on meat and vegetables, while salting fruit and desserts. As the church's liturgical cycle approached Lent, Julia had already reduced the quantity of her nourishment by a third, and soon this became a half. Mamma Maria watched horrified as she began to see the visible effects of these mortifications. In tears she asked, "Julia, what are you doing to yourself? You will ruin your health!"

As a mature anchoress, Sister Nazarena did not boast of these excesses. Over the years she learned to submit every penance to the discernment of her confessors, and she would do nothing without their approval. With ruthless sincerity she confessed, "Before I began these penances, I was quite a patient person; but afterward, doing such violence to myself, I started to show impatience toward others."[33] Another of Julia's nieces, Virginia, who at that time was receiving piano lessons from her, confirmed this judgment. "Julia was very demanding as a teacher," she wrote, "and was impatient with lack of effort and mistakes."[34]

Julia graduated at the head of her class and received the Bachelor of Arts degree in comparative literature and French, *cum laude.*

Easter 1935 marked the first anniversary of the "blessed night." It had remained her secret; she had not confided it to her relatives nor to any of the nuns. Now she decided to search in earnest for the desert to which Jesus called her, and for this she knew she needed help. Again she turned to her sister Rosa and asked to come stay with her in New York. The anonymity of the city would guarantee the secrecy she wished to maintain.

Julia sought advice regarding two points: where to find employment, so that she could support herself and not be a burden to Rosa; and whom to choose as her "spiritual father." Given the tight job market of those depression years, the answer to the second question came easier than the first. Julia was referred to "a certain Monsignor," as she called him, who most likely was Father Thomas Brady, S.J., well known as a spiritual director. Sister Nazarena remembered him with great admiration and fondness: "Even bishops consulted him. It was enough just to see him, to know you could trust him. You could read such goodness in his face. With ease and confidence I opened my soul to him, because from the start I knew he would understand me. Much more! Since his niece, who had been his secretary for the past year, was entering the convent, he was looking for someone to take her place. So it was all settled: I would take over as his secretary. What a grace! In the brief space of an hour, two great needs had been met: a spiritual father and a good job!"[35]

For the first time, Julia narrated her experience of the preceding year and asked guidance in finding her way to that "desert" where Jesus was waiting for her. The goodness of Father Brady kept him from ridiculing her, as some priests after him would do. He did, however, exclude the hypothesis of the Holy Land, the first geographical reference point that came to her mind, and he suggested another place, closer at hand: the Discalced Carmelites in Rhode Island.

Both the priest and Julia recognized that time was needed for reflection. So Julia made a private vow of "abandonment to God's will," meaning complete trust and obedience to her confessor, and went to work as his secretary.[36] After a year and a half, on August 15, 1937, she entered the Carmel of Newport, Rhode Island. The simple fact of living in a religious community, with its regular round of liturgical and private prayer and the austere simplicity of a monastic cell, was pleasing to Julia, and at first the nuns were also pleased with their postulant. But soon Julia was again restless; she told the novice mistress that she felt no clear call to Carmel; on the contrary, she was convinced that she should seek a "real" desert. The novice mistress judged her insane and presented a negative report to the community chapter.[37] This report was later transmitted to the Vatican; it contained the following points:

1. She showed she did not have the personal qualities required for the religious life.
2. She was psychologically abnormal.

3. Her ideas were tainted with the Protestant spirit.

4. Her behavior was often sad and melancholy.

5. Her mind was often subject to delusions.

For the above reasons we cannot in conscience recommend her to any religious community.[38]

Julia left the Newport Carmel on November 6, 1937, and headed straight for New York City. The following morning she called and made an appointment with Father Brady; she asked to speak with him only in the confessional. She did not want him to see her face.

Julia insisted that her only fault was in having expressed herself freely and sincerely to the Carmelite novice mistress and in having said that Jesus wanted her to be alone with him in the desert.

Father Brady upbraided her severely.[39] But then he said, "For the first time in my life I am completely in the dark. I don't know what to say!"

They both remained silent. Julia felt he was praying for light. She was in great pain and begged the Holy Spirit to enlighten him, that he might give her an answer.

Slowly, Father Brady said, "There is nothing I can see for you to do, except to go to Rome and wait there, until God manifests his will for you." Julia was surprised at his words. She asked if she might first visit the Holy Land, to see if it were possible to live in the desert there. The priest replied, "No! You must go directly to Rome."[40] He told her to come to his office later in the day; he would give her a letter of introduction to a fellow Jesuit, Father Edward Coffey, professor at the Gregorian University in Rome.

Julia accepted Father Brady's advice as if God himself had spoken to her. After receiving the priest's blessing, she left the church and went to the passport office to apply for the necessary documents. She booked passage on the first ship sailing for Italy, and wrote a note to her family saying she had left the

Carmelites and was embarking for Rome the following Thursday. She told them that, if she became a religious there, she would never return to the United States, but she said nothing about "going to the desert."

The news of her departure was a terrible blow to everyone at home, and through their tears and their words of affection, Julia could hear their silent reproach. She told them that God had spoken to her through the priest, and therefore she was full of confidence in the face of the unknown.[41]

Her mother and sisters raised no objections. To ease the pain of their good-byes, Maria and Rosa shared with Julia their happy memories of her as a child. Her father said nothing. When the time came for her to leave, she stood to give him a last kiss. As she gazed into his eyes, two large tears ran down his cheeks. He opened his mouth, but no words came out. Julia also remained silent. As she left the house, she looked back for a last glimpse of her mother. Mamma Maria lowered her head into her hands and began to weep bitterly.[42]

Julia Arrives in Rome

On the ship to Italy was a young Jewish woman. Julia began to converse with her and learned that she was returning to Jerusalem. They may have spoken of the persecution of Jews in Nazi Germany. For Julia, the thought of remaining with this new friend and proceeding with her to Israel was a very strong temptation. But her sense of duty prevailed, and she decided to obey her father confessor.[43]

Saying good-bye to her Jewish friend, Julia disembarked at Civitavecchia on December 9, 1937. A short train ride brought her into the city of Rome, where she found lodgings at a *pensione* run by nuns. The following day she went looking for a priest who could hear her confession in English. At the Jesuit church, *il Gesù,* confessors were available for several languages. She told the priest her sins but said nothing about the call to the desert, nor about her having been rejected by the Carmelites. After receiving absolution, she told him she had a letter of introduction from her confessor in New York. The priest took the letter, and seeing his own name on the envelope, said, "I am Edward Coffey."

Father Coffey was a professor of philosophy at the Gregorian University and highly regarded for both his learning and his spirituality. To Julia's first question, whether she could go to the Holy Land and live in the desert, Father Coffey's response was negative; he refused to allow her to discuss the matter any further. The following month and a half were spent making inquiries with various communities, including the Camaldolese Benedictines.

On February 2, 1938, Julia entered the Camaldolese monastery of Sant'Antonio on the Aventine. On Friday, June 24, which in that year marked both the feast of the Sacred Heart of Jesus and the nativity of John the Baptist, she was clothed as a novice. The custom in those days was for young candidates to dress in a white wedding gown with a garlanded veil, which then, in the course of the ceremony, would be exchanged for the monastic habit. The nuns have a photograph of Julia as a bride, taken before the rite, her face illumined with a radiant smile. Another photo shows her as a nun, without a smile.

In fact, she admitted, "I did not feel in place or happy. After a year the ecclesiastical superior decided that I should again enter Carmel."[44] The "superior" was a Capuchin friar, Giovanni Ivo Merli (with the improbable religious name of fra Giovanni da San Giovanni in Persiceto). He was the apostolic deputy for religious, the priest appointed by the Holy See to oversee religious women in the diocese of Rome; he had direct jurisdiction over several cloistered communities, including that of the Camaldolese nuns.

Nazarena did not blame her restlessness on the Sisters at Sant'Antonio. "In spite of the goodness of the community, my soul felt suffocated here. I wondered how much longer I could stand it. Since the way to the Holy Land was closed, the idea of returning to the Carmelites pleased me, but I thought it would be impossible. What is more, I dared not speak of it to the confessor. One day, like a flash, I heard in my soul: 'Enter Carmel again!' I arose immediately and went to tell the novice mistress that I felt I must again enter Carmel."[45]

Padre Giovanni told the story from his own point of view:

> At the beginning of her novitiate, Julia seemed happy and satisfied with the Camaldolese life; then she began to express reservations—she said she found little discipline in the community, a disorderly life, and above all a lack of regular and evangelical silence and none of the solitude she would like. She found it very hard to live the common life and to share in the daily work; she longed for a cell where she could pass the whole day completely alone.... And so she returned to me, insisting that I must absolutely find her a Carmel, if possible outside Rome. I pitied the poor girl! In the face of her insistence and her tears, I begged the prioress of the French Carmel—a monastery of diocesan law and hence under my direct jurisdiction—to allow her at least a long trial period, in order to soothe her tormented soul.[46]

Information about Julia was requested from the Newport Carmel, which sent back the report quoted above. But the French nuns decided to form their own judgment about the American candidate, and in the fall of 1939 they admitted Julia to the novitiate. On November 22, 1940, she made vows as a Carmelite nun.

"If I had only known!" wrote Sister Nazarena. "I was entering a place where the Holy Spirit had kept a great furnace ready for me, blazing hot, and after a few weeks I was thrown into this furnace and left for more than five years, without a single ray of light, without any consolation, comfort, or support, whether human or divine. Complete abandonment, with violent temptations, terrible trials and sufferings of soul and body."[47]

The French nuns called their convent *Carmel de la Réparation;* every ascetical practice was understood as an act of reparation for the sins and crimes of humanity, and every prayer as the payment of a debt incurred by those who do not pray. The cloistered nun was a "victim" who offered herself as a substitute for those on whom divine vengeance ought rightly to fall. Julia was deeply divided between her instinctively positive vision of faith and her desire to conform to the regime of the convent, which Julia realized would be her last chance to make vows in the canonical religious life of the church.

Her suffering at the French Carmel was of two sorts: The first was the continual sense of physical hunger, which seemed worse after eating. One is tempted, of course, to see this as a neurotic symptom; however, these were the years of the Second World War, and in Rome food was generally scarce and of poor quality. Furthermore, Julia was a healthy, athletic woman, who had enjoyed the rich and abundant fare of a well-to-do farming family. The convent rules of fasting and abstinence and war-time privations were enough to cause gnawing hunger pangs in any normal individual. Even so, Julia added her own private mortifications to the convent regime.[48]

The other source of suffering was her difficult relationship with the superiors. The prioress and the novice mistress were from France, while the subprioress was Italian. They were exceptionally severe toward Julia, to the point of cruelty. She later told of the harsh treatment she received from the Carmelites, while excusing them from any personal guilt. "Once the prioress said something to me, which left me with the understanding that they could not have acted otherwise. Without directly willing it, or without being able to resist, they were forcibly driven to treat me harshly.... One must never judge or blame anyone. In the sight of God—only God's judgment is of any value—they were perhaps without the least guilt, since they were unable to do otherwise."[49] Without realizing it, they were "three docile instruments with which the Lord was cleansing me and hardening me so well that I would be able to face any suffering on my own, without any human help or consolation. Neither I nor they had the slightest idea what was happening, but the Lord was secretly preparing me for single-handed combat in solitude."[50] The Italian subprioress later admitted to Julia that she would sometimes think about her at night and weep for what her Sisters had done to her.[51]

The Obstacles Fall

Realizing how precarious was her position in the community, Julia hid her sufferings and uttered no complaints. Nor did she open her soul to the confessor; she would accuse herself of some sins with the minimum of words, and immediately after absolution would leave the confessional. "I was afraid to remain there," wrote Nazarena, "because the nuns made note of how much time I spent in the confessional."[52]

On the eve of her final vows as a Carmelite nun, Julia heard the voice once more, in sweet reproof calling her to the desert.

At this crucial moment, no procedures or formalities were appropriate. She presented herself to the prioress in lay clothing, thanked her for the nuns' hospitality, and walked out onto the streets of Rome. It was the Fourth of July, 1944, and war was still raging outside the "open city." She walked the streets without knowing where to go, stopping at the basilica of Saint Mary Major to ask the Blessed Virgin's intercession. People turned to stare at her—this tall young woman so thin she seemed "a walking skeleton." Julia saw the question in their eyes: "To be reduced to such a state, what great suffering must she have undergone!"[53] Perhaps they thought she had escaped from the Nazi death camps, news of which had just begun to filter through the battlefront. Down the street from the basilica Julia found a soup kitchen run by Sisters; she asked them for a place to stay, in exchange for work. They sent her to the kitchen to peel potatoes, and Julia thanked them for a job that allowed her to remain seated.

The inadequate nourishment and the community tensions at the *Carmel de la Réparation* had brought her to the limit of her physical and psychological strength. Even her heart seemed to beat wearily, and she expected to drop dead at any moment.[54] The good Sisters at the soup kitchen thought, "She seems to have no will to live," but they respected Julia's silence and asked her no questions. Julia took comfort in their discretion and in little else, not even in the thought of heaven.[55] Then to her own and the Sisters' amazement, Julia rapidly began to gain weight, and with the recovery of her physical strength she began to think of her future.

With the arrival of American troops in Rome, the city began returning to normal; shops opened, and dollars circulated, together with the devalued Italian lira. One day a young lady, hearing that Julia was an American, told her that the Allied Financial Agency, which operated out of the Banca d'America e d'Italia, was looking for a secretary fluent in both Italian and English. She went to apply for the job, and the American military officer who ran the agency turned out to be from her hometown in Connecticut; he even knew her nieces. On the strength of Julia's exceptional qualifications, he made her his administrative assistant and put her in charge of the entire clerical staff.[56]

Having found gainful employment, Julia could now turn to her real problem, that of discerning God's will and realizing in some way her vocation to the desert. During her five years at the French Carmel, she had neither sought nor received counsel from a priest. Now she made discreet inquiries and was referred to Giulio Penitenti, a young priest but already a skilled director of souls; he would eventually found an ecumenical religious institute, *Únitas*. Julia's first question—whether she might go to the Holy Land to live alone in the desert, according to the call she had received from Jesus—evoked the usual answer: "Fantasies!"[57] Hearing that Julia had been a cloistered nun for several years, Penitenti contacted Padre Giovanni, expressing an initial judgment of Julia's case that was not entirely positive: "Rather abnormal, with many good qualities, courageous as an Amazon, but with a certain, unexplainable strangeness about her."[58] Nevertheless, the ecumenical priest continued to receive Julia and would listen to her quietly, suspending judgment.

From time to time Julia also spoke to Padre Giovanni, and with him it was a continual tug-of-war. He continued to ridicule her talk of the "desert." Yet he was not entirely convinced of her insanity; might she not indeed have an authentic call to the solitary life? Perhaps the memory of the eremitical origins of his own order, the Capuchins, held him back from dismissing her entirely. His official report of 1952 contains the following admission:

> In the course of the canonical examinations which I was required to administer to Julia, before her entry into the novitiate and simple vows with the Carmelites, I found her always well disposed and ready to accept everything. The superiors were always enthusiastic about her. I saw Julia as a woman with a will of iron, generous, ready and willing to face hard tasks; but also as a fickle and unstable person, who would change her mind from one day to the next.... Never did I receive complaints, for any reason whatsoever, from the superiors and novice mistresses who had her in their care and who sought to favor her religious and spiritual formation. Julia was always docile and obedient, and

in practice, I believe, she sometimes had to exert great effort to obey certain orders which she found repugnant, especially in Carmel, where she met with a very authoritarian superior.[59]

Julia was sincere in her obedience, and in spite of her repeated arguments with priests, she told them she would not make the slightest move without their permission. One day she was shocked to hear her confessor say, "Now you may go to the desert."

She thought he was joking. She looked at him intently; he was obviously serious about what he was saying. Julia replied, "If you are saying this in God's name, I am ready to leave immediately!"

The priest said, "Ah, I cannot accept such a responsibility."

"Nor can I," Julia shot back. "If I left on my own choice, without your permission, the moment I arrived in the desert the devil would start tormenting me, because I went there to do my own will, not God's will."[60]

The discussion returned to square one, and months passed with priest and penitent repeating the same things to each other. The war was now over, and Julia told her spiritual father that if he would not allow her to go to the desert, she would seek admission to another religious community, because she had no desire to remain in the world. If she could not make vows, she would ask the nuns to give her a small room where she could live alone and work for her food.

A few days later, she again approached her confessor with the idea of going to the Holy Land, now that travel in the Mediterranean was again safe. He responded with words of such severity that Julia was reduced to tears. She left, resigned to her fate.

"More than eleven years of this!" she told herself. "What the priests have said must be true: The call I have felt so long comes from my imagination, not from God. I am indeed deluded, insane!" With all the strength of her iron will, Julia resolved to consider any further voice or vision as pure fantasy and as a temptation. She was bitterly unhappy. She had come so far that she felt there was nothing she could go back to, and ahead she could see only a dead end. A mortal anguish laid hold of her soul.[61]

When Julia failed to come for her usual appointment, Penitenti called her and told her to go see Padre Giovanni; he would make arrangements for her entry into the solitary life as a lay anchoress. She feared she was dreaming but hoped against hope that she was not. Her sorrow had suddenly been changed into joy.[62] However, one more hurdle appeared in her path. The Camaldolese would take her back only on the condition that the cardinal vicar of Rome gave her a letter. She would have to request it herself, since neither of the two priests was willing to face Cardinal Marchetti, well known for his opinion that the contemplative religious life was a thing of the past. Julia entered the lion's den alone.

"To my surprise," wrote Sister Nazarena, "the cardinal was very kind and fatherly. Seeing that I had not made a bad impression on him, before leaving I dared ask him if he would permit me to wear a religious habit, should he authorize my return to Sant'Antonio as a lay anchoress. He said yes. When he felt he had asked me enough questions, he told me I would receive his answer through Padre Giovanni. I understood that the answer would be affirmative—and so it was. Thus in a few days, after eleven years of waiting, God's hand stretched forth, and all the obstacles fell. All contrary wills were brought into harmony with God's will."[63]

2. In the Desert

"Miss Crotta, would you like to have a private audience with the pope?" The young women at the Allied Financial Agency gathered excitedly around Julia. The director had just informed them that she would be leaving within a few days to become a religious, and the news that their quiet, discreet, and efficient administrative assistant was quitting her job came as a surprise. "If you want to be received by the Holy Father," said one of the staff, "my uncle can arrange it for you. He is a papal chamberlain. I'll call him now, if you wish."

Julia laughed softly. She expressed gratitude for the offer and told her young colleague, "It's already been arranged! Just a few days ago, a priest came to have supper with us at the *pensione*. We had never seen him before. In the course of our conversation, he asked if I would like to have a private audience—he also has an uncle in the Vatican. I said yes, and he promised to make me an appointment. The following day his uncle asked me what day I would like to be received, and I told him, 'Next Wednesday, November 21, because that is the day I am entering the convent to begin a life of solitude.' This morning a messenger from the Vatican brought me the invitation."[64]

Padre Giovanni accompanied Julia to the office of Cardinal Marchetti, who gave her the papal rescript authorizing her admission to the Camaldolese monastery of Sant'Antonio not as a novice but as a "private recluse," a lay anchoress, to be given a room isolated from the rest of the community for her life of prayer, penitence, and solitude.[65] The cardinal expressed his delight that she would be received by the pope and gave her his blessing. Julia's confessor, Giulio Penitenti, was also present; he told her, "Wednesday morning I'll accompany you to the Vatican and we'll pray at the tomb of Saint Peter."

Julia had begun to draft a rule of life for herself, but Padre Giovanni told her that she was to follow the rules that he, as ecclesiastical superior, would give her in writing, and that she would be required to observe them to the letter for an initial three months' trial period. Julia immediately accepted, and on Tuesday evening, the day before the papal audience and her entry into solitude, he read her the following document:[66]

> Miss Julia Crotta, in virtue of the indult of the Sacred Congregation of Religious, number 3706/45, dated 31 October 1945, enters the Monastery of the Camaldolese Benedictines on the Aventine, there to lead a secluded, eremitical life, in perfect union with God. Such is her ardent desire.
>
> The Anchoress earnestly requests that the nuns receive her purely as an act of charity, and she declares herself ready to leave the monastery in whatsoever moment the Mother Abbess should order her to do so.
>
> She shall remain perpetually segregated from the Community and from the individual nuns, in a separate cell to which no one else shall be admitted.
>
> Every morning she may go down to the Chapel to hear the Holy Mass, and once a week she may approach the confessional of the Monastery.
>
> During the day she may take a walk in the garden or on the terrace. She shall be free to make a visit to the Blessed Sacrament in the Chapel when the nuns are not present. The Anchoress shall take

particular care to have no contact with the Community or the nuns.

She shall divide her day between prayer and work. She shall work for the Monastery, receiving the materials at the door of her cell, in silence, or with a few words if strictly necessary.

She shall be authorized to ask the Abbess for books on spirituality and the lives of the Saints.

Her nourishment shall consist of bread, water, and a teaspoon of oil in the morning; bread, water, fruit, legumes, vegetables, and salad at mid-day and in the evening. She shall follow a vegetarian regime. Her food shall be left at the door of her cell.

Her bed shall consist of simple, rough boards, without straw ticking or a mattress and with blankets as necessary. The cell may be furnished with a table and a bench. On the wall she may have a rudimentary Cross and a modest image of the Immaculate Virgin.

The Anchoress shall dwell in the Monastery as if she were not there at all, ignored by the nuns, and perfectly extraneous to everyone and everything.

In case of illness all the necessary and opportune exceptions to this Rule may be allowed.

The Anchoress freely commits herself to observe this Rule, which was written out in full harmony with her devout wishes, under obedience to the Ecclesiastical Superior, whose consent is required for any future derogations or modifications of the Rule.[67]

Early the next morning, Penitenti met Julia at the *pensione* and took her to Saint Peter's Basilica. They went down to the crypt, where they celebrated the Mass of the Presentation of Mary in the Temple, and Julia remained for a long time in prayer with the priest. She felt that she herself had been the host, offered on the altar for the whole church.[68]

Julia did not attend the usual Wednesday public audience held in the basilica, but with Padre Giovanni she went directly to one of the rooms in the Vatican palace, to await the brief visit of Pope Pius XII.

Shortly after noon the pope entered the room. Julia was awed by his presence and, realizing that she stood several inches taller than he, knelt before him, kissing his ring.

"Your Holiness, this is the rule which I wrote for Julia at her request," said the Capuchin as he handed the document to the pope.

Pope Pius read the rule, then looked up and said to Padre Giovanni, "Isn't it a bit too rigid?"

"I wish it were even more so!" exclaimed Julia.

The Holy Father smiled. "If this is the rule by which you wish to live," he said, "then take it as it is." He made the sign of the cross over the document.[69]

Julia was exultant for the sequence of events that in a matter of days had brought to an end the eleven painful years of waiting. She felt that the entire church, in the person of the pope, had blessed her call to the desert and guaranteed its authenticity.[70] Her conviction was even stronger now than it was at the beginning, after the vision of the Man of Sorrows, because only a short time ago she had decided to release all visions and voices and to accept the priests' unanimous verdict that they were figments of her imagination.

To the end of her life she enjoyed this assurance that her call was the work of the Holy Spirit, while remaining on her guard against self-deception and delusions. "The anchoritic life is the one most subject to delusions and to the crafty conspiracy of its two greatest enemies, the devil and the ego," wrote Sister Nazarena a few months before her passing. "If one has not been severely tested and has not suffered a great deal, there are reasons to doubt whether one could persevere in solitude for very long. From the moment I set foot in the cell, I had no doubts; 'I shall yet have to suffer much,' I told myself, 'but to suffer more than I suffered, all alone, when I was with the Carmelites, I do not believe it would be possible.' I was now well prepared to face suffering and sacrifice, without ever turning back."[71]

Her conviction and her readiness to suffer were put to the test by a curious incident that occurred that very afternoon. Julia took her lunch at Sant'Antonio, and then with Padre Giovanni, the mother abbess, and the prioress, she proceeded to her cell, a room next to the common bath in the lay Sisters' corridor. There was little ceremony. Padre Giovanni sprinkled the room with holy water, gave Julia his blessing, and as he went out, he said, "I now leave you alone, with Jesus, Mary, and the angels."

The door closed behind him, and Julia listened as the superior and the nuns walked quietly down the hall. Then she turned to the cross and the image of the Blessed Virgin and, her heart overflowing with joy, raised her arms to heaven and fell prostrate on the floor. As she rose to her feet, she looked around to see whether everything was as she had requested. She was delighted to note that the bed consisted of two rough planks on a trestle. She bent over to make sure they had been properly nailed together, and as she stood to her full height, she hit her head on the lampshade and bulb and broke them into a thousand pieces. Her joy vanished and was replaced with acute embarrassment. There was nothing to do but sweep up the shards of glass and place them outside the door, together with a note apologizing for breaking the bulb and requesting another.[72]

"Julia's greatest concern was with physical penances," wrote Padre Giovanni. He was wrong, of course, but he did correctly note that she was never satisfied with the rules he gave her, and she never observed them to the letter. Hardly a month passed before she wrote him, signing the letter, for the first time, "Sister Nazarena of Jesus."[73]

She asked his permission to extend her weekday abstinence from cooked food to Sunday as well, and to consume only bread with a few drops of olive oil. She received his consent. "From then on," wrote Sister Nazarena, "I would feel terrible nausea after eating. And it seemed there was a strong voice which gave me no peace, insisting that I was proud and presumptuous, that I was trying to do what only the saints could do, and soon I would see the results: I would end up having to eat meat and endure the humiliation of it. After several days with the nausea and the voice, I wrote to Padre Giovanni again, told him what had happened, and declared that since I had been presumptuous and had failed in humility, I should be ready even to eat meat, if he told me it was God's will. I got a quick answer, and as I opened his letter my heart was racing. What did he reply? To my great joy, he said, 'Keep resisting to the very limit of your resistance!' When I read this, I felt great strength, courage, and hope flow into me. The physical discomfort disappeared, and for years I have been able to continue with only bread and water. God knows how much it cost me, this torment of continual hunger pangs. But may it please him to accept it for the salvation of many souls, who now are blessed with the blessedness of heaven, rather than suffering the torments of hell."[74]

Julia Meets don Anselmo

There is great drama in the story of Julia's quest for the desert and the inner and outer struggles she had to face, before she saw clearly that her call was to the metaphorical "Egypt" implied in the titular saint of the Camaldolese Benedictine nuns in Rome: Saint Antony Abbot, the fourth-century father of Christian monastics. But the drama continued to .

unfold—it is not true, as some have said, that the story ends with her entry into reclusion.

The first letter that, in early 1946, Nazarena wrote to her abbess, Mother Angela Mantrici, insisted on the necessity of making the rule of her reclusion much more clear and definite than the one typewritten page Padre Giovanni had given her. Well-defined rules were not necessary for her, guided and guarded as she was by the Holy Spirit; rather, they were necessary for her superiors. The parameters of her life must be fixed, in order that superiors might not override them with orders contrary to her silence, penitence, and hiddenness.[75]

"May you help me," she wrote, "to be and to remain a walled garden, reserved for him alone, not a public *piazza,* a park where all can walk about and see and know everything. What a farce it would be, to make a solemn profession of silence, solitude, and absolute hiddenness, and then reveal everything, climb on the platform, and put on a show!" Finally she paid her superior the ultimate compliment: "May you be an excellent watchdog for the walled garden of Jesus!" [76]

Shortly after beginning her life as an anchoress, Nazarena met don Anselmo Giabbani, newly elected "procurator general" of the Camaldolese monk-hermits—their representative to the Vatican.

Don Anselmo was born in the Tuscan countryside in the year 1908, climbed the mountain to the Holy Hermitage of Camaldoli and became a monk there at the age of fifteen, and was ordained a priest in France, at the hermitage of Roquebrune near the Riviera. He has been my mentor in the ways of spiritual freedom since I came to Italy from the hermitage in Big Sur, more than thirty years ago.

He was an ambitious man by nature, but he struggled to turn his ambition to good ends. His chief project was to revive his small monastic congregation, which had barely survived a series of civil and ecclesiastical suppressions over the past hundred years. The project depended on the formation of a group of young monks, theologically well trained and open to the new ecumenical currents that were moving in some circles—mainly in France, Belgium, and Germany—where talk of reforming the Catholic Church was no longer taboo. Don Anselmo had an important connection in the Vatican: Monsignor Giovanni Battista Montini, then a high-ranking official of the papal Secretariat of State, he would later become pope. A prudent, soft-spoken diplomat, the future Paul VI had frequented Camaldoli during the 1930s, at the head of a group of young Catholic intellectuals, who after the fall of Fascism would form the nucleus of the liberal "Christian Democracy" delegation to the Italian constitutional assembly.

In the fall of 1945, don Anselmo was elected "procurator general" and went to live at the monastery of Saint Gregory the Great on the Coelian Hill. His duties included those of confessor and advisor to the nuns of Sant'Antonio. On his first visit there, he found a community of devout but poorly educated women, whose only source of income was a small garden and the weaving of crosses and other liturgical ornaments out of palm fronds. The Vatican paid the nuns a paltry sum for their craftwork, which was used in the procession that opened the yearly ceremonies of Holy Week. Anselmo asked the abbess how much the Vatican gave them. She answered, "Fifty thousand *lire*," something like the minimum wage of a manual laborer.

Infuriated, Anselmo went to the Vatican and addressed his complaint to an official in the Congregation for Religious. "What kind of conscience do you people have?" he said. "Twenty nuns with nothing but a garden and no other resources. How do you expect them to live on fifty thousand *lire?*" The official placated his wrath with the promise of a substantial increase in the nuns' stipend. Anselmo then called on his friend Montini. When the topic of Sant'Antonio came up, Montini told him gravely, "There is serious concern here about their future. You must do all you can to help them."

Anselmo returned to Sant'Antonio to inform the abbess of his conversation with Montini, and after they had discussed the community's problems at some length, she said, "An American woman has just arrived—her name is Julia. She hardly eats and always wants to be alone and not speak with anyone." Anselmo asked the abbess to call her down to the parlor.

The anchoress presented herself in a long dress, with a large veil pulled down over her eyes. She muttered her replies to Anselmo's questions, mixing an occasional English word with her garbled Italian.

Anselmo, unable to understand what she was saying, asked her, "*Parlez-vous français?*" He was surprised to hear her respond in fluent French. She asked him, "Please come again tomorrow, Father, because there is a lot I want to tell you."

The following day, the two met privately. Nazarena told Anselmo about her family and her education—music at Yale, then English literature and French. Anselmo was impressed. "This is a highly gifted woman," he thought; "her ideas are clear as crystal." With some hesitation she began telling him the story of her vocation and of the eleven years searching for a place to live it. When she was twenty-six and about to get her degree, she had a vision. Jesus, wounded and weeping, appeared to her and said, "Come with me to the desert!" She was overwhelmed by the experience and came out of it convinced that Jesus wanted her to live in total solitude.

Don Anselmo was taken aback by the story of her vision, but he continued to listen in silence. He was impressed by Julia's strong character, which had enabled her to continue seeking her way to the "desert" even when priests said her vision was pure fantasy or a psychotic symptom. Finally he said, "I have to be certain that you really have this vocation. If you do, you have nothing to worry about, since this is the only order in the Catholic Church where you can live as an anchoress."

She was surprised to hear such positive words from a priest. "Is it really true, Father?"

"Don't worry, Julia," he answered, "but I still need to make sure for myself that this is your calling."

She said, "Yes, Father, whatever you want."

Thus began a lifelong friendship between don Anselmo and the American anchoress. Soon she would write the first of more than a hundred letters to the monk who, from 1946 until her death in 1990, was her confessor and "spiritual father."

Nazarena wrote to Padre Giovanni to inform him that since she now had as her confessor a priest of her own order, she would no longer need his services. He wrote the mother abbess, saying that he had never found her anything but stubborn, willful, and totally undisciplined.[77]

At the Edge of the Abyss

Shortly after meeting don Anselmo, Nazarena wrote him a letter alluding to the accident with the light bulb, the day she entered her cell. Her embarrassment and shame, she said, were like a "healthy dew"; then shifting metaphors, she called them "medicine" for her wounded self-love. "Infinite mercy," she affirmed, "is glorified to the degree that from the most abject misery rises a sightless yet unshakable hope." By herself, Nazarena was and had nothing; all she could offer was what God had given her, a free gift he could withdraw at any moment: limitless hope in God's love and power and infinite mercy, a hope that enabled her to say, as she did time and again during the eleven years of searching, "Now I begin!" This sense of ever-new beginnings in every instant of her existence would sustain her through the days to come and enable her to remain steady in mind and heart at the cross-point of time and eternity.[78]

Her second letter narrated an apocalyptic fantasy she indulged in during the initial three-month trial period of her reclusion. She prefaced her account of the fantasy with the admission that it was probably a "first-class delusion," and that she was writing now mainly to rid herself of the obsessive image of it in her mind.

Between the pages of a book in her cell, she found a post-card of Naples, the famous daguerreotype of the city that showed the fuming, volcanic cone of Vesuvius in the background. A thought flashed through her mind: "Beneath that mountain is hell! Its flaming summit is the mouth of hell, which burns without destroying what it burns. There the souls of the damned plunge into a place of horror and eternal torment!" The image aroused morbid fascination in her, and she speculated that when eruptions occurred, it was to warn sinners that a great number of the damned had fallen therein to feed the flames.

As the macabre thoughts passed, she felt within her a call to fly like an unknown angel to the summit of hell and there, between heaven and the infernal abyss, to seal its mouth with the Eucharistic Bread and Cup. The sacred Species would be, in her hands, a key that would shut hell and open heaven's eternal gates to desperate sinners who otherwise might not be saved. This was to be her secret, apocalyptic mission.

But then she came back to Earth, and dismissing her fantasies and her yearning to hear some echo of heaven's canticles, she expressed her wish to hear nothing, enjoy nothing, see nothing of those marvels that "no eye has seen and no ear has heard, what the mind of man cannot visualize—all that God has prepared for those who love Him" (1 Cor 2:9). She desired that her renunciation of every foretaste of heaven be like a drop of blood in the cup of salvation, to add to the over-flowing chalice of Christ whatever was lacking in his sufferings (Col 1:24)—"a drop from one sinful soul for the sake of other sinful souls." Nazarena concluded with "the thought of saving souls by means of my poor sacrifices and penances, which deserve to be rejected, so defective are they, but...I cast them into the divine cup, 'believing,' and through union with the blood of Jesus all their defects disappear."[79]

The renunciation of her rich fantasy world would not come easily; it would be a lifelong task. Yet from the very beginning she realized and accepted the high price of renunciation, seeing it as her part in the Eucharistic sacrifice of the church.

The Priestly Soul of an Anchoress

About this same time, from the fall of 1946 to her profession of private monastic vows a year later, Nazarena exchanged correspondence with a Benedictine theologian, Father Augustin Mayer, explaining to him the sense she had of being "a priestly soul," involved in the offering of Christ's blood on a par with the church's ordained priests.

Augustin Mayer, later to be an abbot and a cardinal, met Sister Nazarena shortly after her arrival at Sant'Antonio and was deeply impressed with her. To his questions about fostering the spirit of contemplation in an academic environment—he was a professor of theology and student advisor at the Benedictine *Athenaeum* of Sant'Anselmo—she responded with page after page of maxims and counsels for the contemplative quest.

Nazarena addressed Father Augustin with respect but also with great familiarity, greeting him as "my dear brother priest" in her first letter. The anchoress confessed her embarrassment in assuming the role of spiritual counselor; she knew how easily the ego, infecting her good will, could mix valid with misleading counsel. On both sides there was need of humility and docility. Nazarena wrote in haste, to allow as little chance as possible for the ego to raise its head.[80]

The anchoress assessed Father Augustin's spiritual state: "I sense that within yourself you are groping about, that never, since your birth, have you enjoyed the peace and tranquillity of those who are sure they are on the path that suits them." She encouraged him to trust in the guidance of the "two heavenly

Teachers," the Holy Spirit and Mary. Jesus, God's incarnate Word, was formed by the Spirit in the Virgin's womb; priestly souls are formed in like manner. "The Lord wants to be able to count on you; he wants you to have such abundant reserves of the divine life, that it will flow out upon...those whom he most loves and renders fit for the upbuilding of Christ's Mystical Body—the priestly souls."[81]

Of herself Nazarena said, "I also greatly desire, by God's grace, to become like my dear priests 'another Christ,' after my own fashion. May I, like him, in him, with him give my blood drop by drop, but in total hiddenness rather than on the battlefield. Until the end of ages, may I never cease to work for 'all souls' according to this ideal."

Nazarena realized she was venturing onto theological terrain where greater clarity was needed. "Let me share with you my ideal, as you did yours with me. May you offer, together with the sacramental Host, this pristine, hidden host of love for Jesus; humbly ask him to accept and totally transform her, so that she may be made 'wholly divine,' and thus it will be he, not she, who lives and works again on Earth." The use of grammatical gender in Italian renders the identification of the "hidden host of love" with Nazarena herself quite obvious; in other words, through the ministry of the priest, her offering as an anchoress is taken up totally into the sacramental Victim. In the historical work of Jesus, as in its Eucharistic representation, the Victim and the Priest are one, and from this union of the two functions in the one Person, Nazarena draws the following conclusion: "I have no better way of helping 'my dear brother priests' than by becoming like them, a priestess, working and giving my life for the same ideals."[82]

Most theologians would allow little more than metaphorical value to the word *priestess*. Yet Nazarena was not using it as a mere metaphor, an indulgence in literary license. The anchoress, freely offering her life as "a little host of love," added her "drop of blood" to the blood of the new and everlasting covenant in Christ's chalice, consecrated by the ordained priest. Thus she realized a baptismal priesthood in perfect conformity with that of Christ himself and in close analogy with that of his ordained ministers.

There was no doubt in Nazarena's mind that she, a woman and an anchoress, "represented" and "personified" Christ the High Priest "after my own fashion," because she, like him, exercised her priesthood in the offering of herself. After expressing these thoughts to Father Mayer, she shared them with no one else. Only in 1971, writing to don Anselmo, she confessed, "To my astonishment, in a dream some time ago, I saw a woman who was celebrating Mass at the altar!"[83] Nazarena added no comment. Three years later, the prioress of Sant'Antonio began bringing her Communion, and from that time forward, she would receive the Eucharist only from the hands of a nun.

Nazarena's Private Vows

Sister Nazarena and Father Augustin exchanged their last letters on the day of her vows, December 15, 1947.

The authorization she received from the Holy See in 1945 permitted Julia to reside within the cloister of the Camaldolese monastery but gave her no juridical status in the order. Her condition was objectively that of a guest; subjectively, for her and for the community, she was irreversibly dedicated to the monastic state, under those special conditions that guaranteed the realization of her call to extreme solitude and hiddenness.

Monasticism has always posed problems for canonists. Our life cannot be reduced to juridical categories, and in this sense we are not "religious" like other vowed persons in the Catholic Church. Monasteries also have their "oblates"; most are seculars, laity and clergy, whose life of prayer and work draws inspiration from the Benedictine Rule, but some are in all but legal terms full members of the monastic community. The canons of the church may define a religious institute's official "membership" and outward "observance," but monasteries live more by custom than by canon; if a community regards a permanent guest as one of its members, that is what counts in monastic terms.

So it was for Nazarena. When she returned to Sant'Antonio in 1945, after her years at the French Carmel and the year in the world, the nuns rejoiced: "Julia is back!" Her time with them in 1938–1939 had forged a bond of sisterhood that was not broken, only stretched, as Julia searched for her true way. The way led back to the Aventine. Her reentry was understood as a novitiate, a trial period desired by all concerned, and its natural conclusion was the profession of vows.

These were technically private; Nazarena's spiritual commitment to live as a nun was binding on her conscience, not on the community or the church. But that canonical fine point mattered little to the nun who for the occasion inserted four handwritten pages into the monastery chronicle. In florid Italian and fine calligraphy, the anonymous Sister waxed poetic over "Julia's story," her departure from America, even her movements in and out of religious communities. "As it were her will to put human weakness to the test, she spent two years in the Silent Anchorhold before sealing her pact with God, living on bread and water, sleeping on hard boards, and adding to her pains other harsh penances, known only to her soul and to God. But she passed the test, her generous soul did not pull back, and now she wants to advance still further, ascending toward her God, her Jesus who from the naked cross calls her upward and onward."

The chronicler described the profession ceremony with its five vows: poverty, chastity, obedience, solitude, and abandonment. "Today she was clothed in the robe of a hermit—made of pure sackcloth—tailored like the habit of the nuns in this Monastery. Of pure sackcloth was her robe, of Franciscan simplicity the sandals on her bare feet, of plain muslin the veil that covered her visage; as if by her harsh austerity she wished to oppose the soft and easy life of today's unwholesome young women who are trampling on the nobility of the female sex and demolishing by their shamelessness the foundations of our dear fatherland, Italy."[84]

The nun who wrote these lines was projecting her own negative and judgmental attitudes onto Nazarena's intentions, but Nazarena never saw the life of an anchoress in opposition to anyone or anything. It was a positive gift of love, for the salvation of all.

Another Sister, writing to Father Augustin Mayer, narrated with great warmth Nazarena's profession ceremony. "Padre Giovanni was waiting for her at the altar. We sang the *Veni Creator Spiritus* and then he gave a nice talk, speaking directly to Sister Nazarena. Then she came to the altar and pronounced her holy vows. After she had signed the document, we all sang the *Te Deum*. Entering the balustrade of the choir, she embraced the nuns warmly, one by one—this was really moving! She was beautiful as sunshine, smiling and standing tall and on fire with a great love of God!"[85] As different as the two narratives are, they express the sentiment of great affection and admiration for Sister Nazarena shared by all the nuns.[86]

The Hard Labor of Love

Nazarena did not reflect on the fact that she was forty years of age. The reclusion and the vows were more a departure than an arrival for her. Throughout her letters, like the refrain of a responsorial Psalm, she repeated the Latin phrase *Nunc coepi,* "Now I begin," from the Vulgate mistranslation of a Hebrew verse recited weekly in the Divine Office. But something had been settled within her, not only in her outward circumstances. Doubts would arise in the coming years, restless moments would afflict her spirit, misunderstandings would drive thin wedges between the anchoress and her Sisters; yet the greater weight would remain on the side of her stability at Sant'Antonio.

Sister Nazarena's perseverance would be due, after the grace of God, to her candor and honesty in expressing her doubts promptly to her confessor and her abbess. She held nothing in, nor did she project her own problems on others. While not scrupulous to the point of neurosis, Nazarena had a hypersensitive conscience, and she requested guidance and permission for certain things that a "normal" person would decide on her own.[87] Padre Giovanni criticized this constant questioning in Nazarena and even ascribed it, paradoxically, to a rebellious spirit. He may not have been entirely wrong. According to his mentality, she should have abided by the *Regolamento* he had given her, followed the letter of the law, and asked no further questions. But there can be no final law for an anchoress.

During the months preceding her vows, Nazarena jotted down notes for an anchoress's rule. When she was ready to share these jottings with her abbess, Mother Angela, she typed everything out and sent the notes with a covering letter. "As I wrote," she told the abbess, "I was not looking at the order or the style, as you will see. I noted down many more points than what would be necessary for a rule. I wrote extensively to give you a broad basis for judging whether my deepest motivations, my ideas, and my aspirations are sound and healthy, and whether they ought to be followed, in whole or in part. I would be glad if you could set me at ease on this and advise me, so that I can feel secure in reclusion."[88] Nazarena expected her superiors to organize the material into a formal rule, because it was to be binding on both—she was ready to obey, but she wanted the special nature of her vocation to be acknowledged and guaranteed in writing. "Since I feel that I have done my part, now the responsibility falls to you."[89]

Nazarena's notes followed the outline of Padre Giovanni's one-page *Regolamento*. The opening lines declared her will to renounce "visions" both internal and external. "To love, to suffer, to keep silence, alone with God alone, without seeing anything, without feeling anything, without enjoying or knowing anything of the results of her self-sacrifice for love.... To live and to die solitary and unknown, not only to others but even to herself."[90]

She expressed concern lest she be drawn out of her hiddenness and solitude even by correspondence: "The anchoress may communicate with superiors and her confessor only as necessary. Every spiritual conversation or exchange of letters will be forbidden."[91] In a sense, Nazarena did observe this last point, cutting off the correspondence with Father Augustin; however, she continued to write extensively to don Anselmo and a few others.

Prayer, the ultimate *raison d'être* of an anchoress, was to be totally free and charismatic. "Perfect liberty to follow at each moment the inspirations and attractions of the Holy Spirit. No obligatory vocal prayers."[92] She did, however, mention the Divine Office or Liturgy of the Hours, which in accordance with the ecclesiastical mentality of the day she considered one of many optional vocal prayers. Eventually she would begin reciting the Hours, and after the Second Vatican Council she would adopt the Italian Office with the rest of the community.

Nazarena provided detailed specifications for fasting and corporeal penances. Her paragraphs on work expressed her understanding of the spiritual and material value of laboring with her hands. "To obey the divine precept of earning one's bread by the sweat of one's brow and in a spirit of charity, to give a helping hand to the community which hosts her and to which she owes so much, she shall have a fixed work program with a production deadline; she shall dedicate a determined number of hours to work every day.... She shall make a special commitment never to allow herself a single idle moment nor to waste one minute of time."[93]

It came as a surprise when don Anselmo told me that

Nazarena sometimes worked as much as twelve hours a day. Later, reading her letters to the abbess, I discovered occasional complaints about the heavy work load. Nazarena was not entirely justified in her complaints. The Camaldolese constitutions prescribed only two hours' work for solitaries, but she chose to burden herself with extra tasks, especially during the weeks preceding the deadline for the Holy Week palms. Nazarena intended the extra toil as a labor of love for her Sisters, who were delighted. "Nazarena does the work of two nuns," they would say, perhaps forgetting that she ate half as much as anyone else.[94]

Her statements about work were traditional and echoed similar expressions in the Rule of Saint Benedict. But in the way she practiced manual labor, one can see the unconscious contamination of her spirit by the "Puritan work ethic." For the sake of work, Nazarena set aside regular meditation, spiritual reading, and the peaceful course of her daily schedule, especially as the annual Holy Week deadline drew near. Could there have been something of the workaholic in her? In this respect she can be compared with Thomas Merton; the Trappist poet and essayist had the reputation of being a "pure contemplative," and yet he must have spent most of his waking hours at work, since at his early death he left a literary inheritance of some sixty volumes.

To these typewritten pages, Nazarena added some handwritten notes. One of them expressed her desire to have one of the Camaldolese monks as her immediate superior. Clearly, she wished to withdraw from the authority of Padre Giovanni, who, while he respected Nazarena's courage, remained convinced that her desire for a solitary life had pathological and not supernatural causes.

Nazarena's Solemn Monastic Profession

"For the soul a door opens out onto a new way of life, indeed to a new life, in which the freedom to give herself to the Lord is truly absolute." Nazarena wrote these lines to don Anselmo shortly after her profession of vows, in response to his request for a statement of her theological understanding of the anchoritic life. She formulated her understanding in two simple points:

> 1. The greatest glory a person can give to God is to let herself be invaded and filled with God's love, and the greatest title of glory and perfection a religious order can enjoy is to facilitate and predispose the maximum freedom for God and souls to enter into this mystical union.
> 2. On a social level, even one single act of contemplative love, or the attainment of a higher degree of union with God, is of greater value than all other works put together.
>
> Upon these principles, carried to their ultimate consequences, is based the anchoritic way of life, widely misunderstood by many and thought by some to be utter madness, but which on the contrary stands as the holiest expression of the Christian apostolate and as a magnificent commentary on the dogma of the Communion of the Saints.[95]

Nazarena's sense of belonging to the Camaldolese continued to deepen, especially as she felt a fresh wind blowing in the congregation. Don Anselmo conversed freely with the anchoress and shared with her the program of *aggiornamento* by which he was trying to favor that kind of liberty within a plurality of monastic forms which Nazarena believed to be essential for an authentic contemplative life.

In 1948, Mother Angela Mantrici concluded her term of office, and the nuns had a new abbess, very much in favor of Nazarena's presence in the community, Mother Scolastica Berardi. During the next four years the abbess and the anchoress would be corresponding frequently, although only a few of Nazarena's letters of that period have been preserved. Those we have regard her desire to withdraw from Padre Giovanni's direction and to become a full, canonical member of the community. Mother Scolastica consulted him and received the following reply.

> I tell you quite frankly that if Sister Nazarena wants to withdraw from my direction and place herself under someone else, I couldn't be happier. Certainly, I should not take the initiative myself, fearing to go counter to the will of God, who entrusted this soul to me many years ago. But if this is what she wants, let her do it.
>
> Nazarena is a burden to me and a cause for serious concern, because she is an original, eccentric soul, abnormal in every sense: a genuine pathological case. She cannot bear any sort of discipline that might demand the renunciation of her own will. She has this fixation, that Jesus speaks to her and guides her personally.
>
> From the start I realized that this was the case, and so I adopted the tactic of bringing her down to earth gradually, while avoiding head-on collisions. Now that she sees that she must practice obedience and renounce her strange ideas, she believes it would be to her advantage if someone else directs her. Let her have her way. All the better for me, since it takes a weight off my shoulders.
>
> If the Vatican authorities wish to interrogate me, let them call; I shall be happy to give them all the information and help I can. But if they do not, I shall say nothing, out of consideration for you. However, you would do well to remind Nazarena that the late Cardinal Marchetti did not want the superiors to get involved with her, and that he considered her to be

just a guest of your monastery, like the other ladies who were living there at that time.[96]

Nazarena was neither surprised nor discouraged by Padre Giovanni's letter. She wrote serenely to Mother Scolastica, expressing her desire to profess public vows, which of course would require permission from the Holy See. Nazarena was confident that her abbess and don Anselmo would obtain it.

"You already know what Padre Giovanni thinks about this," said Nazarena. "He believes I should stay as I am, a private solitary.... Padre Giovanni believes he knows me well. But I think you, Mother, know me even better, and you are better able than he is to understand my vocation. If I am not mistaken, God has also given you the desire to see me become a nun-anchoress, not just a lay-anchoress."[97] Nazarena's desire for solemn profession was not of recent date, but she had hesitated to take steps in that direction, for fear it was just another delusion. But the desire had grown stronger, convincing her that it was inspired by God.

Nazarena knew her own mind. She knew she was not abnormal, but she did confess to having "a proud, vain, and presumptuous nature" that needed to experience trials and humiliations and failures. But "now I feel quite broken," she said. "In my soul there is but one, immense desire: to bury myself in a cell as in a true desert, a desert inaccessible to everyone, to be alone with God and to offer myself as a holocaust for souls. To live and to die an unknown solitary. But as a solitary nun! With solemn vows, I wish to make a clean break, once and for all, with everyone, and to begin at last the life God is calling me to."[98]

Mother Scolastica began to make inquiries. Padre Giovanni promised to raise no objections, if the Holy See did not ask his opinion. The abbess wrote to Giulio Penitenti, who had guided Nazarena during the year and a half after she left the Carmelites. He replied:

It is praiseworthy on Nazarena's part to desire to be incardinated into the order. I think you should proceed as follows: you obviously cannot follow the canonical procedure, since she lacks the canonical title for solemn profession, that is, the novitiate and temporary vows. Hence you must appeal for an exception, on the grounds that her whole existence is exceptional. I advise you to write a brief letter to the Cardinal Vicar of Rome, informing him of the form of life—extracanonical—Sister Nazarena has been leading, with the approval and blessing, however, of the Holy Father. Inquire whether a special privilege might be granted her, with a papal dispensation from novitiate and simple profession, in order that she might make canonical vows.[99]

On receiving Penitenti's advice, the abbess wrote the Holy See, declaring that she and the entire community had expressed their favorable opinion in a chapter vote. The letter was dated July 5, 1952; and although the answer would be long in coming, Nazarena remained in deep peace, confident that at last her vocation would be publicly and definitively confirmed by the highest authority in the church. The papal dispensation arrived in the fall, bearing the date November 7, 1952. Nazarena reminded the abbess that this was the fifteenth anniversary of that morning in New York, when in the confessional Father Brady told her she must go to Rome and wait there, until God made known to her his will.

3. The Anchoress and Her Sisters

Nazarena did not immediately make her vows on receipt of the papal dispensation. She chose to finish weaving the Holy Week palms and to spend Easter in prayer to the "heavenly Teachers," the Holy Spirit and Mary. Then, on the octave of Pentecost, Trinity Sunday in the year 1953, the thirty-first of May, Sister Nazarena of Jesus, baptized Julia Crotta, finally and forever became a Camaldolese Benedictine nun at the monastery of Sant'Antonio on the Aventine. However exceptional her vocation, henceforth she would live it within a community of monastic women who were emerging from a season of material and spiritual poverty, and yet were heirs to a remarkable history.

The nuns were convinced that Nazarena belonged with them. Only in their constitutions, they told her, was allowance made for the "singularity"—or madness!—of total reclusion. Instinctively she knew they were right: God had made their paths cross, and although doubts would later assail her, Nazarena never again thought of changing communities.

In addition to the constitutional basis for the anchoritic life, there was a deeper reason for the affinity between the anchoress and the Camaldolese Benedictines. The three-hundred-year history of their community in some way foreshadowed Nazarena's search for the desert. They had begun as a lay movement, without canonical status or rules of cloister. They moved from one house to another in Rome until, after the death of their foundress, Mother Angela Pezza, they inherited the property of the Knights of Saint Antony of Egypt on the Esquiline. Their peaceful, cloistered existence there lasted only thirty years. In 1809 Napoleon's troops descended on Rome and established a secular government that disbanded all women's monastic communities. Only a handful of the nuns survived, ensconced in the palace of a Roman noblewoman. After the restoration of church properties, the nuns returned to their ruined house on the Esquiline, but in 1871 the community was again suppressed by the "liberal" Italian government of Cavour. This time the community held together, and for six years they survived in various temporary shelters, until the Holy See purchased a modest villa on the Aventine hill, which today remains their home.

The courage and tenacity that brought forty-six women, eighteen to eighty years of age, through six years of homelessness had exhausted their collective energies. The original community, driven out of Sant'Antonio on the Esquiline, persevered together to the end, but postulants were fewer and fewer as the years went by. The Great War, harbinger of the atrocities that burden the conscience of twentieth-century humanity, affected them in ways that the simple nuns could hardly understand. In 1918, Italy found itself on the victors' side but bore collective wounds worse than those of the defeated Austrians. Practicing Catholics held aloof from politics, but when Benito Mussolini's totalitarian ideology came to power, with promises that the Fascist government would settle the "Roman question"—the papacy's role in secular Italy — most ecclesiastics applauded.

Threats of expropriation did not cease with the nuns' arrival on the Aventine. In the first year of Mussolini's dictatorship the government decreed that a monument to the nineteenth-century *Risorgimento* leader Giuseppe Mazzini be built in the nuns' garden. A breach was made in the wall, a platform was erected, and the first stone was laid, to the accompaniment of military bands. The nuns cowered in their chapel, its windows darkened with penitential drapery. Nothing further was done, however, as other interests captured the attention of the Fascists, and eventually the monument was set up in the municipal rose garden nearby.

In the years between the world wars the climate at Sant'Antonio was that of continuing crisis. The nuns found themselves in a state of spiritual disorientation, with no clear ideas about the nature of monasticism as it came to them from the Benedictine Rule and the traditions of Camaldoli. The ecclesiastical jargon of the day defined their collective depression as "laxity" and "a lack of regular observance." The nuns' financial misery led Vatican officials to entertain the hypothesis of closing the community in Rome and assigning them to other Camaldolese monasteries. Monsignor Montini brought this prospect to don Anselmo's attention the first time he came to the Vatican, on assuming office as procurator general of the monks in 1945.

Warned of the danger of one more suppression, the nuns decided to ask a member of another, more vigorous community to assume the role of abbess and undertake a general reorganization of the life at Sant'Antonio. In 1948 Mother Scolastica Berardi arrived from the monastery of Poppi in Tuscany. A strict disciplinarian, she was impressed with the American anchoress and saw in her a silent ally in the work of reintroducing the "full regular observance" among the Sisters. In 1955, Mother Scolastica retired into a semi-eremitical life, and another nun from Poppi, Ildegarde Ghinassi, came to assume the office of abbess.

Like most cloistered women in those days, Mother Ildegarde had little formal education. Yet she was an avid reader, and during her youth at the monastery in Tuscany she educated herself beyond the levels of most of the Sisters. She had not the extraordinary intellectual or artistic gifts of her namesake, Saint Hildegard of Bingen, but like her and like Saint

Gertrude the Great she developed a deep life of prayer centered on the liturgy and the sacramental mysteries.[100] Quite as capable of exercising authority as was Mother Scolastica, Ildegarde was also gifted with a fine pastoral sense, and as the Benedictine Rule exhorts the abbot, she sought "more to be loved than to be feared."[101]

Letters to Ildegarde

On the feast of Saint Hildegard, September 17, 1955, Sister Nazarena sent greetings to the new abbess, enclosing a few small crosses woven of palm leaves and adorned with silk flowers. These simple, affectionate words initiated thirty-five years of correspondence and collaboration between the two extraordinary women. They would alternately counsel and guide each other in a respectful, give-and-take relationship, and would both leave their mark on the community.

The first year of the new abbess's mandate proved difficult. Some of the nuns hesitated to accept the young, reform-minded superior. In a moment of discouragement Ildegarde shared her woes with the anchoress. Nazarena replied with generic words of comfort, but a short time later she felt impelled to write again.

> Reverend Mother, you are a good soldier—strong, generous, courageous, and persevering. Now work on being a joyful one, to fight with holy joy and never let yourself become downcast or discouraged, come what may. Discouragement does not come from Jesus but from self-love and from the devil. It clips your wings. Joy fortifies the soul and keeps her from losing heart. It will give you the courage to lift your foot and step over the stumbling blocks on your path, big or small, and keep walking.

Do not be too demanding with the novices. Keep in mind that they are in the novitiate in order to learn how to practice the virtues; don't expect consummate virtue from them. Learn how to work with each one as a unique person, helping her to know her own defects and work to overcome them. Be evenhanded with everyone. If a novice makes no more than one single step, this is already a great leap forward!...

You have great liberty of spirit, but work on increasing it. Regarding spiritual direction, let me repeat what I said: In my experience both Jesus and the spiritual father are pleased to see a soul open her heart and speak with the greatest freedom and sincerity....

I don't expect you to take seriously what I wrote here—give it only the attention you feel it deserves.

Enlarge your heart, and run in the way of Love.[102]

The day after sending this sensible advice to the abbess, Nazarena wrote another letter to say she regretted that she had assumed a role—that of counselor—which was not rightfully hers. These acts of repentance were quite common in the correspondence with Ildegarde. The anchoress expressed herself with spontaneity and frankness and then repented of having done so. "Forget everything I said yesterday," she wrote. "Since I haven't the grace of state to be your counselor, I can get everything wrong.... Like a real Sister I was trying to help you, for your own good and that of the community, but I would have helped you more had I kept to my task: praying and sacrificing in silence and hiddenness." Having said this, Nazarena could not resist adding another word of advice. "The Lord has to give you superiors the light to know his will, the only thing that counts. He will never fail to give you his light,...provided you act with a clear conscience, humility, and abandonment, and you know how to wait and keep praying when the light doesn't come and the Lord does not act—this is just a sign that his hour has not yet come."[103]

In 1958 Mother Ildegarde's first term of office was due to expire; neither she nor the anchoress was certain of the abbess's reconfirmation. Nazarena wrote her in the late spring, shortly before Pentecost. "I want to take the occasion of a change of superiors to launch myself with greater generosity, fervor, and courage into my life as an anchoress, which up to now has fallen short of expectations. I want everything to be well regulated, as far as you and the father general are concerned, so that I can be sure I'm obeying you. Once everything has been well arranged, I hope and believe I shall hardly ever have to disturb either of you—it is my desire that you will need but rarely to check up on me; for a real anchoress, 'God alone' ought to be sufficient."[104]

Mother Ildegarde was confirmed as abbess; she would remain in office for the rest of her long life.

Foundations and Reforms

From the beginning of her anchoritic life, Nazarena was drawn into community dynamics, precisely because she had chosen as her confessor don Anselmo Giabbani, who from 1945 to 1951 was procurator of the Camaldolese monk-hermits and then, after 1951, abbot general. Like Ildegarde, Anselmo was a reformer. He faced opposition from those who were adverse to change as such, and from those who misconstrued his concern for the human and cultural formation of the younger monks, fearing that Anselmo's "monastic humanism" would undermine the solitary observances that characterize the Camaldolese hermitage. The tensions in the Catholic Church that marked the paradigm shift canonized by Vatican II had their effect on our monasteries and hermitages as well, especially when don Anselmo, an assiduous reader of

French, began quoting theologians like Henri de Lubac, Yves Congar, and Jean Daniélou, then under clouds of suspicion in conservative ecclesiastical circles.

Halfway through his first term in office, don Anselmo engaged the mechanism of constitutional reform in the congregation. The Camaldolese *Constitutions and Declarations* are not exclusively a legal code; they are rather a commentary on the Benedictine Rule that adapts its spirituality to the life of the hermitage and of the "eremitical coenobium." Revision of the constitutions was not an end in itself. Both Anselmo and Ildegarde were planning to found new communities. The publication of Thomas Merton's writings in Italian had given the Camaldolese the idea that Saint Romuald's hermit ideal might have a special appeal for Americans. The revised legislation, they hoped, would expand the horizons of the congregation, geographically and intellectually, beyond the provincial confines of north-central Italy.

In 1957 don Anselmo, reconfirmed in office for another six years, informed Sister Nazarena that he was going to the United States and asked her advice. She sent him several pages, an Emily-Postish code of manners on how to deal with Americans. "While traveling in America, work at keeping your tone of voice down, and avoid moving your body too much when you speak—always and everywhere move with dignity and composure, without haste. Doing this should help you achieve inner self-control, recollection, and union with God."[105] Reminding him that the Rule of Saint Benedict barely tolerated wine, she warned him that Americans do not respect priests who smoke and drink liquor. Above all she recommended that he pay great attention to the way he celebrated mass. Nazarena voiced strong complaints to Anselmo, as earlier she did to Augustin Mayer, about priests who "parrot" the words of the liturgy, rather than praying them, slowly and attentively. "Praying the mass is the most beautiful and efficacious sermon that a priest can give."[106]

Nazarena added further advice, perhaps foreseeing the accusations against don Anselmo, which, in his absence, would reach the Holy See. "The priest who is slow in granting generous and ready forgiveness, who wastes his words on detraction, who succumbs to the pettiness of gossip, resentment, vindictiveness, moodiness, and all such miseries of self-love, to such a priest Jesus will certainly not grant an increase of charity. He may even withdraw his ordinary assistance, and thus the priest will remain all his life poor in grace and charity, wallowing in self-pity."[107]

Anselmo returned from the United States without having decided on a location for the new monastery. He was also without the flowing beard he had worn for his entire adult life. This change in his outward image perhaps contributed to the polarization that was lacerating the community of Camaldoli. At the Hermitage in Tuscany was a former Jesuit who, having lived for many years in Australia, spoke fluent English. This was the man whom don Anselmo sent, together with the assistant general don Aliprando Catani, to find land for a hermitage in the United States. Entrusting the American foundation to the former Jesuit was one of many instances in which Anselmo's holiest vice, his ingenuous trust in people, caused him immense disappointment. Charged with finding property for the American Camaldoli, the ex-Jesuit arranged to have don Aliprando, his traveling companion, sent back to Italy, and then set himself up with the bishop of Fresno, California, as the founder of "The Camaldolese Hermits of America."

Anselmo immediately recalled the "founder" to Rome and had him expelled from the order. But the imbroglio in the United States gave the Holy See one more reason to launch an investigation of Camaldoli and its general superior. The Vatican congregation for the Doctrine of the Faith (then called the "Holy Office," the name by which the Inquisition had once been known), sent an "apostolic visitor" to prepare a report on Camaldoli and its daughter house in Big Sur. The allegations against don Anselmo reached the ears of Monsignor Montini, then archbishop of Milan, who wrote him a very harsh letter. Anselmo immediately went to Milan to explain the matter, but Montini received him coldly.

Returning to Rome, Anselmo went to Nazarena's cell, sure that she would understand him. Once again, the usual roles of priest and penitent were reversed. He told her of the deep hurt the loss of Montini's friendship caused him. Sister Nazarena gave him words of comfort but not cheap consolation: "If the treasure hidden under insults and contempt were manifest to us, we would nurture a special love for those persons who occasion them. In heaven we shall grasp fully how unimportant are earthly honor or disgrace." She criticized his defensive attitude and his self-pity: "The anxiety about defending your 'honor' and your 'talents' makes it impossible for us to include you among the ranks of those who regard such things as 'refuse' and who are glad to lose themselves in Christ."[108] Anselmo remained in office for three more years, determined to guarantee the survival of New Camaldoli. He succeeded, of course, but success gave him no satisfaction. The bitterness of his humiliation continued to gnaw at his soul.

The Cell

The life of an anchoress, as distinct from that of a hermit, adds to the traditional penitential practices—fasting, night vigils, and so forth—severe spatial restriction. While itinerant preaching and pilgrimage are not incompatible with the eremitical vocation, the desert calling of anchorite or anchoress leads him or her to a condition of extreme physical confinement. Hence any small room in a monastery, as at Sant'Antonio on the Aventine, can be adequate for the anchoritic life.

Sister Nazarena moved from one room to another during her first years at Sant'Antonio. Then in the fall of 1959, she entered a cell on the third floor where she would remain until her death thirty-one years later. In a letter to the abbess, after a few requests for the arrangement of the cell, Nazarena said, "I wish to be the most hidden and least-known soul in the world—truly and totally 'hidden with Christ in God' [Col 3:3], immolating my whole being together with Jesus, for the love of God and of souls. Oh, how strongly I feel this desire! If you, the father general, and the community help me to do this, your reward will be guaranteed. You will see the great change in me…. May the anchoress's cell be a blessing for the entire community! As for me, I am all the more aware of how unworthy I am of my vocation. I owe the Blessed Virgin, Mother of mercy and divine grace, for all the mercies and graces I have received, which I have not merited in any way."[109]

It occurred to Nazarena that it was inappropriate to move into the new room without rewriting her rule of life. She even postponed the move, in order that don Anselmo might come and examine what she had written. As always, Anselmo quickly read her notes and granted permission for everything, knowing full well that the anchoress would in any case follow the Holy Spirit, not her written rules.[110]

The anchoress recognized her need for support in this new phase, and she wanted the nuns of Sant'Antonio to know what affection and gratitude she felt toward them. "Tell them I salute them all with a sisterly hug in the Spirit, and I hope to stay close to every single one, with my poor prayers and sacrifices. Would that I might help them all to love and carry their cross of everyday sacrifices with holy joy, so that they may sanctify themselves and help in the sanctification of souls, day by day. May we love the blessed cross of Jesus. This is how we store up treasure in heaven!… I'll be glad, Mother, if you don't tell any of the nuns I'm moving to the new cell before I'm there (I can't believe it's true!)."[111]

On October 11 Nazarena moved in. After a few days she wrote Mother Ildegarde, confessing that although the new arrangement gave her "immense joy," it pained her that she could not spend more time working on the palms. She asked the community to accept the diminished productivity on her part as a sacrifice for the greater good of her call to contemplative prayer.[112] The following year, in a long letter outlining her program for Lent, she specified the precise number of pieces she would weave for the Vatican, but it is clear that even so, the work would occupy most of her waking hours, with time left only for the recitation of the Day Hours of the Divine Office. The search for balance between prayer and manual labor continued throughout the year; it would remain a recurrent theme in her letters.

Nazarena's Christmas letter of 1960 opened with a curious passage about dumplings, because for the feast-day dinner, the Sisters sent a large plate of them to her cell. "I am grateful for the kind thought," she wrote. "However I humbly beg you not to send me any more dumplings. For two reasons: first, because long ago I made a sacrifice of both dumplings and desserts and asked the Blessed Mother to give them to Jesus as a gift from me. Second, because the present *Regolamento* forbids them. So yesterday I was embarrassed, because if I ate the dumplings I was breaking the *Regolamento* (which, since it has been blessed by the competent authority, I am obliged to obey), but if I didn't eat them I would be disobeying you. So that I won't become scrupulous and also won't break the rules or take back what I offered to the Blessed Mother, please do not send me any more dumplings.... I hope you understand. One who is not willing to give her all and forever, limited only by her weakness, should not try to be an anchoress. In her cell she will not find God, but only herself and the misery of the ego."[113]

Nazarena was convinced that one of her predominant vices was gluttony, although anyone else would probably have called it the naturally hearty appetite of a tall, athletic woman. Knowing Nazarena's positive, sometimes playful personality, one can see a touch of self-irony in the letter about the dumplings. On the other hand, overzealous mortification of the palate did for a brief period lead her to the opposite extreme of scrupulosity and anorexia. Early in 1961 she began to suspect that she had exceeded the prudent limits of fasting. "As I am vanity and pride personified, I cannot believe that the Lord wants me to live without eating. Perhaps he has in store for me a fine humiliation, as I deserve, and we shall see that my going without food is a purely natural phenomenon, in no way supernatural.... May the Lord protect me from blind self-deceit, and from deceiving you or the monks with all my chatter! This is what I fear most, and I almost regret having spoken to you about it at all."[114]

A Women's Hermitage

"This Easter it is twenty-seven years since the call to solitude rang loudly in my ears; now God is making me hear it louder than ever." In 1961, at the end of Lent, Nazarena wrote to the abbess, expressing the happiness she had found in reclusion.

> My soul finds its place and feels holy peace only in solitude. Whenever I leave it, I feel restless and spiritually unable to breathe. Strange, but true! Perhaps Jesus permits me to feel this way in order to make it absolutely clear that he is calling me and wants me to cling to him alone in the strictest solitude....
>
> I do so love my religious family—now that everything is settled, I want to pray more and better for you. I always feel ashamed when I offer my poor prayers! But I unite them with the merits of Jesus and thus I hope they will not be altogether useless.... I am glad I have no knowledge of any person or event, outside of what is strictly necessary for me

to know. Please do me this kindness, that all my mind and soul may be filled with God and souls, without any particular knowledge of them. I shall better avoid distractions if I know nothing about persons or events. In any case I feel I have to do this, whether I want to or not. When the Lord wants certain things, he gives you no rest until he has them![115]

By 1961, the American hermitage had a new superior, Clement Roggi, and under the gentle but watchful eye of don Aliprando, Anselmo's trusted assistant, New Camaldoli had begun to attract young men, myself included. It had also attracted disaffected individuals from other religious congregations, who found there an "ideal set-up," one of them told me, "for getting away from the active life."

The report on New Camaldoli that reached the Vatican described a flourishing foundation, more zealous and enthusiastic about the hermit life than the mother house of the congregation in Italy. The report posed a dilemma for the "Holy Office": how to remove don Anselmo without undermining the American foundation. The solution was don Aliprando, who at first refused to accept but finally, with extreme repugnance, agreed to exchange offices with Anselmo. Aliprando's gentle mien would eventually defuse the explosive situation, and within another three years nearly everyone at Camaldoli would be saying, "Don Anselmo was right after all."

With Sister Nazarena the correspondence continued as before, and don Anselmo, now free to dedicate more time to writing and to the new communities, began to recover from his disappointments. The nuns were examining projects for new monasteries in the United States and South Korea. About the latter, memories at Sant'Antonio are vague. We can reconstruct the sequence of events as follows: A Korean-born superior of a missionary congregation had a niece—Nazarena called her

Susanna—who longed to see a contemplative monastery for women in her country, which, with its Buddhist tradition, already held the monastic ideal in high regard. She and another woman were willing to come to Sant'Antonio and receive their initial formation; then, if all went well, they would return to Korea and found a monastery of "strict observance," with some cells for hermitesses.

Nazarena's reaction to the project was ambivalent. "I was surprised," she wrote to Anselmo, "that the Mother had told me nothing before talking to you about it. I hope she has no intention of getting me involved." It seemed natural to call on Nazarena to guide the Korean postulants, since in Korea, English was taught in many schools. In fact, don Anselmo had already broached the issue with her. Nazarena's answer was categorical: "I feel I must humbly tell you, my spiritual father, in whose hands are my soul and my vocation: The sense of certitude I have admits not the least doubt that I, in this monastery, must have nothing whatever to do with anyone or anything outside of living alone with God alone and doing my work.... If ever I were to have anything to do with this matter of Korea, it would be there, in Korea. Here in Rome, absolutely nothing. I wish you would find some way of conveying this to the Mother, because I would rather she did not count on me, not even for the least thing, because it is not God's will that I get involved."[116]

Her answer was categorical, but with a small loophole. Under certain precise conditions, she might consider taking part in a foundation. "Would to God it were his will that the foundation be initiated there, in Korea, without bringing any candidates to Italy or anywhere else."[117] If the foundation were begun directly in Korea—not in Italy or the United States—then Nazarena might consider going there, to live her life as an anchoress within the Korean community. In the last paragraph of the letter, she even betrayed a certain enthusiasm: "In Korea, before starting anything else, if only you could build something according to plans well thought out in view of the diversities of context, so that it would be a model for other foundations, if God so willed and gave his blessing. How many ideas I would have about this!"[118] Nazarena did not use the word *inculturation,* not yet common in ecclesiastical parlance, but it is clear that this is what she was talking about.

The Korean project never got beyond the talking stage, because at the same time the prior of New Camaldoli was receiving requests from American women for the foundation of a community along the lines of the Big Sur hermitage. Replying to a Poor Clare nun, he informed her that an American woman, living as an anchoress in Rome, would of course be the prioress or novice mistress of the new foundation. When Nazarena was asked to translate the correspondence, she felt trapped. She left out the reference to herself, but then, tormented by her conscience, she apologized by voice and by letter to the abbess and don Anselmo.

Nazarena accompanied her apologies with open criticism of Mother Ildegarde's decision to invite two American women—identified in Nazarena's letters as "R." and "B."—to come for initial monastic formation at Sant'Antonio. "They have decided that the Americans are to come here. It pains me, but I respect their decision. I hope they do not want me to do anything. To be sure, I told the Mother that if they come I cannot speak to them.... How much it pains me! But I am not able to suffocate the voice of my conscience, which orders me to say, with humility, 'I cannot.' Father, is there really any place for my vocation in a religious order? No! That is, unless limitations are placed on the authority of superiors over my soul and my vocation. It has always troubled my conscience, this struggle between obedience, which means losing my vocation, and suffocating the clear, strong, certain voice within. Sooner or later this will have to be settled, for the tranquillity of my conscience."[119]

The twentieth anniversary of Nazarena's presence as an anchoress at Sant'Antonio—November 21, 1965—gave her an occasion to remind the abbess of what she had just written to don Anselmo. "So as not to keep repeating the same thing over and over again, let me state firmly and for the last time what I have already told you several times: I must have absolutely nothing to do with the American women." But she did add: "The foundation is dear to my heart. I think and pray about it, but I don't want to get involved. May the Holy Spirit enlighten you and the superiors!"[120]

On Ash Wednesday, February 23, 1966, Pope Paul VI paid a brief visit to Sant'Antonio. Sister Nazarena received his blessing at the door of her cell, her veil as usual covering her eyes. The pope's words to the community, extolling the hidden life of prayer and penance and its value for the mission of the church, seemed to Nazarena the confirmation of what she had written in November.

Letters arrived from R. and B., and Nazarena was asked to translate them. The fact that the American candidates knew little Italian caused the anchoress misgivings, and she reiterated her intention to remain "firm as a mountain." The two Americans were "dear" to Nazarena, but she intended to treat them the same way she treated her own nieces, that is, without any contact or correspondence other than the spiritual connections of prayer. Any other contact would only "poke holes" in her vocation and give scandal.[121]

In the end B. never came to Italy, but R., who was already a religious, entered Sant'Antonio and established a close friendship with Sister Nazarena. However, the nuns set aside the American project for the time being and founded a monastery in Africa, in the south of Tanzania near a village called Mafinga. Today the monastery is flourishing; it has also become the nucleus of a new village population, guided by the nuns not only in their religious faith but also in the practical organization of their life. The nuns of Mafinga are living an experience of

Benedictine implantation similar to that of Anglo-Germanic monasticism, when Saints Lioba, Walburga, and Thecla, companions of Saint Boniface, evangelized and instructed the German peasants more than a thousand years ago.

The African foundation merits a book to itself. In 1968, the bishop of Iringa in Tanzania invited the Camaldolese monks to his diocese. The superiors sent the novice master, a former missionary, to investigate the possibilities. On his return it became clear that neither Camaldoli nor the Big Sur community had the personnel or the means to attempt a foundation. At that Mother Ildegarde came forth and, to solicit volunteers, declared that she herself was ready to resign and leave immediately for Tanzania. "If we give birth to a monastery in Africa," she asserted, "it would be worth even the death of Sant'Antonio."

Three nuns eventually responded to Ildegarde's call, and the two eldest accompanied the abbess on her first trip to Africa, there to remain. The third and youngest, before joining her sisters in Africa, would be the recipient of nine letters from Nazarena, in response to a series of questions about the spiritual life.

A Season of Restlessness

When the Catholic Church entered her season of renewal, the era of Pope John XXIII and the Second Vatican Council, Nazarena was drawn into the process. The council was about being "up-to-date": In the popular mind, *aggiornamento,* "updating," was its central theme. Sister Nazarena perceived Vatican II as an event that involved her, inasmuch as she was part of the church. At the end of the council she obtained an English translation of its documents, and among her papers are the notes she took as she read them. Closest to her was the liturgical reform, which the nuns of Sant'Antonio, encouraged and counseled by the Benedictine professors at the nearby Liturgical Institute, adopted willingly.

Nazarena expressed a generally positive judgment of these innovations, along with a few doubts. She was pleased that the nuns were praying in Italian rather than in Latin, and that while the structure of the Divine Office was now more simple, the community's prayer had been enriched with a greater variety of readings, prayers, and vernacular chants. "In comparison with the new Office," wrote Nazarena, "the old one seems antique and out-of-date."[122] She expressed some concern that the simpler nuns might experience difficulty in keeping abreast of the others, finding their place in the new books, and so forth. "As for myself, I would omit a few little things, but I am quite happy to recite the new Office as it is, to conform myself to what the others are doing."[123] In fact, she was opposed to any idea of going back to the older liturgical practice; to do so, she said, would show a lack of willingness to collaborate with the reform program of the council.

And then, as usual, she followed up her letter to the abbess with a note apologizing for involving herself in matters about which she had no competence.[124]

In line with the council's ecumenical spirit, the nuns extended their guest ministry toward persons other than the devout Catholic pilgrims who came to visit the Eternal City's basilicas and catacombs. Sant'Antonio entered into an agreement with a liberal-arts college from Nazarena's home state of Connecticut. The nuns would host the students in the "junior year abroad" program; most of these young people would be non-Catholics. While maintaining a discreet rule of cloister, the nuns could not but feel the contagion of the students' energy, and the labor involved in preparing meals and running the guest house kept most of them quite active. Hard work was necessary to maintain a level of income sufficient for the support of the African foundation. The nuns also decided to found a monastery in Dallas, Texas.

The climate at Sant'Antonio had changed markedly from what it was in 1945. Had Nazarena voiced criticism of the "active life" that seemed to have overtaken this cloistered, contemplative community, no one would have been surprised. And yet there was no such criticism on her part. In her letters we find only expressions of concern, lest the hard work weigh too heavily on her Sisters. However, she does allude to differences of opinion in the community about her own way of life. A few of the nuns, prompted perhaps by don Anselmo, were saying the time had come for Sister Nazarena to collaborate more directly, not only with manual labor—she never failed to "pay her way" by weaving the palm-crosses for the Vatican—but now with community formation. Ought she not to accept the office of novice mistress (perhaps the nuns were thinking of Thomas Merton's example), now that the former novice mistress, Sister Emanuella, was to be prioress of the American foundation?

When the possibility of a Camaldolese women's community in America reappeared on the horizon, it awakened in Nazarena the pain of exile. Faithful as she was to her call, a certain involuntary restlessness now troubled her spirit. Nazarena was delighted by the presence at Sant'Antonio of the young American Sister, who spoke of her dreams of a hermitage for women, modeled after New Camaldoli in Big Sur. Soon this sister—who received from Nazarena the name by which she was known in the monastery: Maddalena—made her vows, and after a few months she requested permission to live as an anchoress herself. She remained in reclusion only a few months. Mother Ildegarde called Maddalena to her office and showed her a stack of letters from potential American candidates for a Camaldolese nuns' hermitage. The abbess ordered Maddalena to accompany Sister Emanuella to Dallas; before leaving, Maddalena promised to build Nazarena a cell in the new hermitage. Nazarena wrote enthusiastically to don Anselmo.

You can imagine my joy when I saw your letter and read it. Oh, will it ever be true that I shall have that cell I have been longing for, these many years? What it does to my soul, just thinking about it!

Did you write Sister Maddalena? Tell her that if she builds the kind of cell my vocation requires, and which here it is impossible to build, I shall be more than grateful, and pray more than ever for her and the foundation. I'll be a true Sister for her, working for the community without bothering any-one. Once everything is set up, my needs will be minimal....

To return to the United States! I never would have dreamed of doing so! A new foundation with hermit cells, and an anchoress's cell "just for me!" I can't tell you what I feel in my soul. How the possi-bility puts everything in a new perspective! I feel I must go, but I do not see clearly what is waiting for me there. I have the feeling there will be something great, but almost everything about it is mysterious and unknown—I do not see or understand every-thing. At the time willed by God, God will unveil the particulars about this feeling that "I must go." Normally God will light up one step at a time, rather than the whole road.[125]

"I never would have dreamed," wrote Nazarena, of return-ing to the United States. In fact she never did, because soon Maddalena was back in Rome. Two Italian nuns remained in Dallas; the few women who came to join them proved unfit for monastic life, and the project was abandoned.

By the mid-seventies Nazarena was questioning, not her call to the desert, but her stability in the monastery and in the institutional religious life of the church. She seemed to find an answer: "I must leave!" Yet she placed both question and answer before God in prayer and before don Anselmo and Mother Ildegarde in a series of long and tormented letters. Nazarena preferred to think of leaving, rather than criticizing her Sisters for their "activism" or invoking a return to the "strict observance."

Maddalena remained close to the anchoress. Nazarena confided in her and confessed she was uncertain whether she could continue to live her desert vocation at Sant'Antonio. Nazarena's doubts were occasioned in part by her increasing sensitivity to the cold; although freezing temperatures are rare in Rome, the rainy Mediterranean winter can chill one to the bone. Advancing years and her unremitting practice of fasting and abstinence began to take their toll. In spite of this, Nazarena held fast to her practice.

To Maddalena she complained about drafts: "I do not know how much longer I will have to wait before the roof will be fixed," she wrote. "Even then, it is uncertain if they will succeed in preventing the drafts. Remaining here then will ruin my strong health. I am feeling more and more the effects of the drafts. Rather than going to another cell and having to go out for mass and other things, I will leave." Realizing that her complaint was too selfish, Nazarena immediately corrected herself: "Let us see God in all that he permits and accept all with confidence and hope. He never fails souls who put all their trust in him, although he may try them much. The Mother does what she thinks best for the community and according as she feels. She is most generous in giving all that she will give you. We must never judge anyone. Before God, they may not be at fault. All depends upon the intention with which we act."[126]

The "chilly drafts" became an obsession for the anchoress. She kept writing the abbess about them, and these long letters, painful to read, revealed an unacknowledged conflict within her, unconsciously expressed through her physical symptoms. "Mother, I really cannot sleep in my cell any more. Now I'm getting congested. What makes me sick is having to breathe all that cold air that comes down from the ceiling all night and fills the whole cell."[127] She made various suggestions: getting a carpenter to nail boards over the plastered ceiling, or putting heavy tape around windows and doors. The nuns suggested she add some wine and cheese to her diet. She replied, "I am returning the wine, and I have made the firm resolution to hold the line and not take anything other than what I usually take (unless I have a very high fever), in spite of the great nausea I feel eating nothing but bread and water and in spite of my great hunger for something extra (what a relief it would be for me!)." But the resolution to keep her strict fast, she said, gave her "peace and joy."[128]

In January 1975 Nazarena began a letter to Mother Ildegarde with affectionate New Year's greetings, but then launched into complaints about the chills and physical pains that tormented her nights. "Mother, I cannot go on living here," she said, "because this would ruin my robust health."[129] Nazarena feared, with good reason, that were she to become an invalid, she would be taken out of reclusion. "Look at the condition I'm in!" she exclaimed. But then she added, "I have the feeling, Mother dear, that behind all this are Jesus and the Holy Spirit. In spite of everything I have to trust and surrender to them. I feel strongly that by Palm Sunday things will be clearer. We shall see a little better what is God's will for me. For now, I have to give myself to prayer and listening, while I finish my work."[130]

As her discomfort intensified, the only alternative seemed to be the renunciation of the anchoritic life—which was no alternative, since her call to the desert was beyond all doubt. Nazarena began to wonder whether God might be sending her a message. Could the Spirit be telling her that she was no longer to live her vocation at Sant'Antonio but must search elsewhere? But where? "If I have to leave the cell, it isn't reclusion any more! I am faced with a painful choice: I shall be compelled to leave the monastery, because here I cannot remain in reclusion without having to leave the cell. Sometimes I get the feeling that Jesus is permitting this in order to force me to leave here and arrange my life and vocation once for all outside of any religious order, because no order can allow for my vocation. I cannot follow the rules and constitutions of any order, since no rule is suited to my vocation; nor can I give superiors the liberty (which they ought to have) of freely making dispositions in my regard, because that would soon lead to my being called out into community life, and this would ruin my vocation." As she did once before, in a letter to don Anselmo, she stated her dilemma in the most drastic terms. But having done so, she immediately reaffirmed her love for her Sisters: "Dear Mother, I love the community — I love it so. To leave here is unthinkable, and yet this is what I keep feeling more and more!... Help me to do God's will, whenever it shall please God to make it clear (I have the impression it will be soon, before or after Palm Sunday). Present conditions are painful, but I accept them with joy, because Jesus doesn't want us to accept what is painful with sadness or by force. I thank you so much for all you have already done for me. May Jesus richly reward you. I send you a hug."[131]

Nazarena was walking a razor's edge. Her will was growing weaker now, just as her formerly ramrod-straight physique had started to bend and shrivel under the weight of her nearly seventy years. A tone of bitterness crept into her long and confused letters.

> I have no Camaldolese vocation. Over these many years, experience has shown me that staying in an order without a vocation but only according to stipulated conditions, uncertain whether they will be respected, rather than favor my vocation does the contrary. Hence it is my firm resolution to leave the

order as soon as I have finished the work on the palms. I shall start my life all over again in a little room somewhere, where I can live my call to the full, in the strictest silence and hiddenness, without fear that I shall be obliged to go anywhere.... May Jesus tell you all the rest that I am unable to say. May he grant you and all the Sisters many, many graces.[132]

Nazarena felt remorse for her bitter words as soon as she sent the letter to Mother Ildegarde. She wrote again, and tore up the letter. A third attempt at baring her soul was prefaced with a cautionary paragraph and concluded with a more careful statement of her dilemma.

What I said last winter about God's will had nothing to do with my calling as an anchoress—never, since I have been in reclusion, have I been tempted to abandon it. The uncertainty which has been troubling me for years regards only my continuing membership in the order—stipulated under certain precise conditions which may or may not be respected—without my having an authentic Camaldolese vocation. Am I to live the last years of my life and calling here? When and as the Holy Spirit wills it, a decisive light shall be shed on this question. As I wait for this, I feel I must do what I said: give myself totally now to an anchoritic life pushed to its extreme limits....

The more I withdraw into God and with God into silence, the closer I feel to everyone and the more I find everyone. The more I make my little efforts to help others by practicing my calling, the more fruit I bear, albeit without seeing a single fruit. I must live my life with naked and pure faith, giving everything without seeing anything.... What holy peace and joy this gives to my soul! Even if all I

give is worth no more than a penny, how pleasing it
is to God, because what counts is the slightest effort
to give one's all, and how great is the reward: God's
all!

Forgive my defects and faults. A hug for you and
all the Sisters.[133]

This painful correspondence continued for a year or two.
Work was done on her room, insulation was put in, and then
something happened that Nazarena called "hard blows to my
blind and mindless presumption and pride."[134] It is useless to
speculate on what these "blows" were—an inner realization, an
outer event, or both. They may have some connection with
Maddalena's departure from the community in the summer of
1977. The shock may have awakened Nazarena to her own
frailty of body and spirit.

> I was stunned and in darkness, impotent and greatly
> pained. Only now am I starting to recover and come
> to my senses, and can see a bit more clearly. Oh,
> what deep and blessed peace comes when you touch
> your own nothingness, misery, impotence, and
> weakness! What do human efforts avail, if they are
> not sustained by grace? I thought I understood this
> and a lot else, but now I see that I understood practi-
> cally nothing. Deep in my soul I feel that great
> changes have begun and are taking place.
>
> I am totally unworthy to be in this cell, but never-
> theless here is the place where Jesus wants me to
> be. Never have I felt so strongly the call to live alone
> with Jesus alone.... I'm recovering now, and I feel
> energy, hope, fervor coming back to me, to begin
> anew the solitary climb, after this painful lesson. (It
> was terrible! What temptations to despair, day and
> night! I felt unable to go on!) Now I have learned
> how totally unworthy I am of reclusion, that I am

nothing but a mass of misery, defects, weaknesses, cowardice. Because of this I feel deeply grateful to God, to the community, and to the order for bestowing on me this grace which I do not deserve at all. But along with this gratefulness there has to be an ardent desire to start all over again, and to ask with all my heart the grace of a new beginning, without taking anything for granted.[135]

Another letter, which most probably followed on the heels of the preceding, gives us a clue to the "blow" that reawakened Nazarena to her own human reality. It involved the realization that her complaints about "chilly drafts" and physical aches and pains had led her to criticize her Sisters, and that she went so far as to blame them for the uncomfortable conditions in which she herself had chosen to live.

How easy it is to slide back down the slope and to lose all the ground one has gained with such great effort! Up until recently I never dared to speak ill of anyone—I preferred to suffer. And now, how easily I let myself do it! I am blind, and I complain about others' blindness! How easy it is to be blind and delude and fool oneself!...

May the Lord be blessed for teaching me that salutary lesson, and for infusing into my soul such a deep and lively repentance. May these graces be the start of my true, complete, and permanent conversion!...

Mother, forgive my many faults, weaknesses, miseries! Forgive the continuous scandal I have given! And pray with and for me, for the grace and strength to make up for everything and start all over again! With Jesus and Mary, give me your blessing, so that I can take a step forward and repay the same grace for my Sisters. Let me not waste any more time, God's grace, my vocation, my life!

With deep gratefulness I thank you with all my heart for all your goodness and patience with me. May Jesus turn all you have done for me into unceasing blessings for your soul.[136]

4. Final Freedom

"What a misfortune it would have been if I had left." Mother Ildegarde sighed as she read these words in a letter from the anchoress, dated July 1981. "When you came today, I was thinking of saying nothing. How I thank God that I did speak! When I heard you say how sure you were—after I had explained everything—that I must remain faithful here at whatever cost, what joy and peace I felt, and still do! Now I know for sure that God wants me to stay faithfully in this cell, in spite of whatever I suffer here. I understand that it was the devil making me feel all those fears.... Now and then I still do get ideas about Jerusalem or other places. I think the Holy Spirit permits this, wanting me to be open to everything, to go or to stay wherever the Spirit wills. How clearly I am beginning to see that so far I have been an anchoress in name only, ardent in desire but poor in effort! How well God's light dissipates the darkness of my spiritual ignorance and blindness!"[137]

With this clarity Nazarena entered the last decade of her life. The light had come to her like the answer to her quest for the desert. In the fall of 1945, after eleven years of searching, after five, painful years at the *Carmel de la Réparation,* and after the latest rebuke from her confessor, Julia decided to release her vocation entirely. The very day she admitted that what she saw in the Paschal night of 1934 was only a dream, that the voice that said, "Julia, come with me to the desert" was a projection of her unconscious mind, as she was about to leave Rome and return to the United States, the priest called to say that he had arranged for her to enter Sant'Antonio as a lay anchoress. Now, once again, having recognized her human frailty, Sister Nazarena went forth into the vast, open space of freedom in the Spirit of God, while remaining in her little room on the third floor of the Camaldolese monastery in Rome.

She wrote, "We need to avoid trying to offer God what is beyond our strength at the moment." Vanished was the illusion of accomplishing great things by force of will; Nazarena now saw that, in the spiritual life as in art, less is more. "Jesus looks especially at the love behind the offering. He is pleased more by one, leftover crumb offered with joy, love, and faithfulness, than by a rich dinner offered by one who is impatient and sad, having exceeded her present limits. We must go forward with humility, little by little; this way, the soul is strengthened and gains courage."[138] Close to her fortieth anniversary in reclusion, the anchoress saw herself "still far from holiness.... But I am not discouraged. 'Now I begin!' I 'hope against hope' [Rom 4:18]—how dear to me are these divine words of holy Scripture. And the mercy of Jesus is without limits. His grace has all the power of God."[139] Nazarena identified her own offering with the widow's coin (Mk 12:42), not with the fasting of the Pharisee (Lk 18:12). "Not quantity, but quality! Only one thing does Jesus want: our heart, the great treasure of the soul. Neither our brains nor our big works. 'Where your heart is, there is your treasure'" (Mt 6:21).[140]

Again and again she repeated these biblical phrases, these themes of mercy and hope and grace, in her notes to Ildegarde and the Sisters during the last ten years of her life. At the head of almost every one of the last letters, she drew a simple cross, with an eighth note at the four extremities. She never wrote the music that—in the estimation of David Stanley Smith at Yale—she had the talent to write. Her music had been her life as an anchoress, a "love song" that almost lost its melody in the dissonance of her crisis in the 1970s, but that attained resolution in the four-note cadence of her final years.

A younger contemporary of Julia-Nazarena, an American composer who said he did not believe in God, wrote: "I do believe in the belief in God when expressed believably by plebeian practitioners or revolutionaries, or fantastically by saints and artists.... Reiteration of faith is suspect to infidels: it never seems to go beyond itself, but proves itself only through the self-hypnosis of that very reiteration, not through good acts. A believer is narrow, an artist is wide."[141]

Sister Nazarena was a true artist. Her belief was wider than the world itself, and her good acts, though hidden, were good indeed.

Opening the Bible

On the twenty-first of November, 1988, the forty-third anniversary of her entry into reclusion at Sant'Antonio, Sister Nazarena addressed a letter to don Anselmo, the abbess, and her Sisters, "my heart overflowing with gratitude," she wrote, "first, to God, and then to the community and the order."

> Thinking about what to say, I had the feeling I should just take the Bible and pray to the Father, the Holy Spirit, Jesus, and the heavenly Mother to guide me in opening it to a few passages which would be a special word for each of you. The Bible speaks to us if we read it with lively faith and gratefulness for the great, divine gift. Almighty God stoops down to talk with the littlest creature. Can we ever thank God enough for so great a gift?...
>
> These many years in blessed solitude I have been alone with God (and with, in, and through God I have been with you all, and shall be "until time is no more"). Holy Scripture has been my greatest

support all along. Even now, under the hard blows that make me open my eyes, it is even more so. Usually it is our Lady—my dear heavenly Mother—who speaks the hard words, because she wants to show me how far I am from the blessed summit; she wants me to quicken my steps and become more generous—our generosity attracts God's generous gifts of grace.... With God what counts is a holy intention, together with humble, continual efforts in spite of a lack of success, relying always on God's strength. God's mercy and almighty love have no limits![142]

Another small note, probably included with the preceding, gives a series of biblical verses, as it were messages from heaven. Nazarena has no need of visions or mysterious, inner voices. The voice of holy Scripture inspires and guides her now.

From the Father: "I bless You, Father, Lord of heaven and of earth, for hiding these things from the learned and the clever and revealing them to little children." [Mt 11:25]

From the Holy Spirit: "Unless a wheat grain falls into the earth and dies, it remains only a single grain; but if it dies, it yields a rich harvest." [Jn 12:24]

From Jesus: The Lord says: "Look, I am standing at the door, knocking. If one of you hears me calling and opens the door, I will come in to share a meal at that person's side." [Rv 3:20]

From the heavenly Mother: "Whoever invokes me will receive my answer; in distress I am at that person's side." [Ps 91:15][143]

When Nazarena quoted Scripture, she never gave the chap-

ter-and-verse citation, nor did she comment on it. She offered
single verses, phrases or words, not as proof-texts, but as illus-
trations of her inner experience. She gave us these biblical
words as keys to her life, for they were the support and solace
for her whole existence as an anchoress. More than once she
took up, as if they were her own words, those uttered in the
Psalms by the Lord of Israel—for example, in Psalm 132:14.
She placed the verse from Psalm 91 on the lips of the Blessed
Virgin Mary.

Nazarena's use of Scripture had nothing in common with
scholarly exegesis. It was not even, properly speaking, theological, except insofar as the anchoress's life with God was itself a
locus theologicus. Hers was an intuitive, sympathetic, and
esthetic approach. The Bible, even when it is "the Law" and
"the Word of God," is above all poetry and story, implying
music. The unbelieving composer, whose paradoxical credo I
quoted above, has all his life given melodies to biblical texts
and prayers. His first song was an Alleluia. Nazarena's life was
an Alleluia; she put both her talent and her genius into her life.

Nazarena's Last Letter

On the seventeenth of January, 1990, the Solemnity of Saint
Antony of Egypt, Nazarena sent a feast-day message to the
community.

> To my dear Mother, to the Prioress, and to my Sis-
> ters,
>
> Best wishes for a happy feast day. May Jesus bless
> you with a double portion of grace.
>
> Instead of my own, poor words, I send you divine
> words from holy Scripture.
>
> Here they are: "Yes, I know what plans I have in
> mind for you—the Lord declares—plans for peace,
> not for disaster, to give you a future and a hope.

When you call to me and come and pray to me, I shall listen to you. When you search for me you will find me, when you search wholeheartedly for me" [Jer 29:11–13]. A beautiful passage! May it please Jesus to find a happy attention in each one of you!

I keep myself always closely united to you. I hope you have a little thought for me.[144]

In Paradisum

In August 1989, Mother Ildegarde was in Africa, and the prioress of Sant'Antonio, Sister Scolastica, was acting superior. For the feast of the Assumption of Mary, she brought the anchoress a bouquet of flowers to set before the image of the Blessed Virgin in her cell.

They exchanged a few words on spiritual matters. Speaking of the end of her own life, Nazarena said, "I wish to die alone, like Saint Romuald."

"No, Sister Nazarena," replied Scolastica. "You have been alone all your life. But when you die, your Sisters want to be with you." As it happened, the Lord honored the wish of the nuns of Sant'Antonio: The whole community was present at Nazarena's passing into eternity. However, the anchoress did die as she had lived—in total surrender to the Lord and in profound, mystical communion with her Sisters and all humanity.

By custom, the nuns of Sant'Antonio invite their Camaldolese brothers at San Gregorio to come for Vespers and supper on February 10, the feast of Saint Scholastica. In 1990 this date fell on Saturday, and for liturgical reasons it was decided to anticipate the celebration. So on Wednesday the seventh, the memorial of Saint Romuald's entombment at the church of Saint Blaise in Fabriano, the monks and nuns were together for the evening prayer and meal. A bishop from Brasil presided at the liturgy; he had come to invite the nuns to found a monastery in his diocese.

That afternoon, Sister Ilda was working in the *lavoriero* just outside Nazarena's room. As she was about to leave, she heard a soft knocking inside the cell. Seeing the door ajar, she looked in. Ilda had nurse's training, and immediately realized that Nazarena was close to death. Mother Ildegarde came, and seeing that the anchoress, who could hardly remain upright, had no chair in her room, insisted that she allow a bamboo armchair to be brought. "It has no padding or upholstery," the abbess said, anticipating Nazarena's objection. The doctor came, saw there was nothing he could do, and left.

After Vespers, the abbess looked in again. Since the anchoress was still conscious, the abbess went to take supper with the community. Lest she trouble the festive occasion, the abbess did not publicly announce Nazarena's grave condition but whispered a few words to don Anselmo, who discreetly left the refectory and went to her cell. In the meantime, Sister Lucia was assigned to remain with the anchoress while the nuns were in the kitchen washing dishes. Don Anselmo entered and seated himself on a low, wooden box in front of her. They looked into each other's eyes for the first and last time.

Nazarena reached out and grasped Anselmo's hands. "Father, I'm not well," she said.

Anselmo answered, "The doctor said that your heart would fail if we moved you to the hospital." His voice choked with emotion, he tried to comfort her: "Soon you will be with Jesus."

She said, "Please bless me."

Don Anselmo placed his hands on her head, recited a blessing, and made the sign of the cross on her forehead. Sister Lucia started to leave, but Anselmo called her back. "Stay with her—I'm afraid she won't last the night." He left the room and returned to San Gregorio.

Nazarena was uncomfortable in the armchair—she never sat on anything except her low stool. As soon as she was alone with Lucia, she suddenly stood up. Lucia looked at her with astonishment. Nazarena's face was white as bread, but with a luminous smile. Lucia asked, "Where do you want to go?" The anchoress summoned her last energies and began to move toward the large wooden box with the raised cross on its lid, where every night for the last thirty-one years she had taken her usual three hours of rest. Lucia assisted her faltering steps. As soon as the anchoress reached the box she collapsed and lay across it, her feet still touching the floor.

Confused and anxious, Lucia said, "Nazarena, you're too sick—you can't stay here! Let me put you back in the chair, and when mother abbess comes she will tell us what to do." She carried Nazarena back to the armchair. There she remained, calm and silent, for her few, final hours on earth.

By that time the nuns had heard that the anchoress might not live to see morning, and they went to her room. They found her awake, and she gazed at them silently, with bright eyes. A couple of hours passed. The nuns were singing Psalms; all of them wished to remain until the end. They began a hymn—an Easter song, with verses written by one of the monks, for which I had composed the melody. The nuns had just sung the last verse, and with the words "Amen, alleluia," Nazarena sighed and rendered in perfect silence her soul to the Bridegroom. She saw Jesus for the second time, and forever.

"I in You, You in Me"

"Sister Nazarena will end her life with one last act of love for her heavenly Bridegroom," said don Anselmo shortly before her death. Nazarena performed that act of love when she dragged herself over to the wooden box with the cross on its lid. Having done so, she died to her own will. "You could even say she died alone," Lucia told me. "I was nothing but a crutch for her." During the anchoress's last hours, each of the nuns saw her in a different way: One saw her "fighting the last battle"; others saw her in sweet surrender to the Lord. But when she gave out her last sigh, they all said, "We beheld the resurrection."

When don Anselmo first met Nazarena, she was wearing a veil. Two hours before she passed away, the veil was lifted, and they looked into each other's eyes for the first time.

Anselmo said, "When I saw that Nazarena's door was open and the Sisters were milling about, I asked her, 'Do you want to be left alone?' She said no. I realized that she was happy to have the community share in her dying, because it was a stupendous passage into eternity."

"The only time you looked into each other's eyes was during those few minutes?" I asked. "The nuns described the scene for me: It was like two old friends saying inarticulate good-byes as one of you was leaving for a journey. Familiarity and simple affection..."

"What else would you expect?" said Anselmo, a bit brusquely, trying to hide his emotions.

"The nuns told me you were holding hands."

"It was the only time we ever did! When Nazarena was dying I did not even give her absolution; I felt there was nothing to absolve. Since the nuns were there, singing Psalms and hymns, I withdrew. However, we remained connected. After an hour and a half, she passed away, and I was immediately aware it happened. I said no prayers for the repose of her soul. Being in deep contact with her, I felt her enter directly into the glory of the Lord, without any need for purification. Nazarena was so penetrated with the mystery of Christ as to be totally one with him—all I could think of were Jesus' words in John: 'I in you, you in me.'"

I remained silent. Don Anselmo smiled. "Now Sister Nazarena is your friend too, Thomas."

"I am certain of it, don Anselmo. I always felt she was there praying for me without knowing me. Or maybe she did know who I was."

"As her confessor," said don Anselmo, "I knew more about

her than you did. But just as she desired to remain hidden to everyone except God, so I also, for the sake of prudence, held back my own curiosity. Our friendship had to remain strictly spiritual. I did not see her face, but I saw the crucifix on the wall.... She used to say, 'Father, you are responsible for my soul; remember that I take everything you say as coming from God.' So I had to be careful with what I said to her, and obviously, being her confessor, I was bound to absolute silence and could say nothing to others. But I can say this: For more than forty years I was witness to her sincerity, her loyalty, her consecration to the Lord, who was the ground of her existence and to whom she was determined to remain faithful. I can tell you one thing about our friendship, which up to now I have kept as a private matter. Nazarena wanted to be a second guardian angel for me. That is, she wanted to be spiritually close to me in whatever circumstance. Over the years I experienced her presence, and I still do. She said she would do this out of gratitude for me, her confessor and superior. I hope she will help me when my time comes, and that we will all be together in glory."

PART TWO
Questioning Nazarena

✝

Those of us who knew Sister Nazarena, either personally or by sharing the same monastic life as Camaldolese Benedictines, may have an image of her different from that which others form, reading the story of her life as an anchoress. I hope my account will not make the reader see her as some kind of ascetical freak, even though "heroic." Nazarena saw herself as an ordinary person, called by God to live humbly in a little space, doing her daily work and prayer for love's sake. She had no delusions of grandeur, and we would be deluded, I think, if we projected grandeur onto her life.

Although she chose to be hidden and inaccessible—even to herself—she was capable of recognizing the need for consolation in those with whom she spoke or corresponded. Then she would listen willingly and speak freely, often for hours. Don Anselmo knew her for a longer time than anyone else, but probably her abbess, Mother Ildegarde, knew her more intimately. I had only begun to study Nazarena's letters, when—in March 1993—the abbess suddenly died, in church, as she led her Sisters in procession at the hour of Vespers. Hence I was unable to interview her, although I do remember a number of anecdotes and reminiscences about the anchoress that, over the years, Mother Ildegarde shared with me.

The following year, I interviewed don Anselmo at length. He spoke of many things, not only of Nazarena. Occasionally his memories were blurred, or his accounts of past troubles among the Camaldolese were self-serving. But he was unquestionably sincere, even though the truth as he saw it might be contested by others who saw things differently. In the following pages I have tried to distill the essence of his experience with Nazarena, for whom he was the "spiritual father" but from whom he received more guidance than he gave.

1. Conversations with Don Anselmo

We are in an infirmary room at Camaldoli, where Anselmo is spending the summer of 1994. He was close to death a few months ago, but now he is back on his feet. His wits and his tongue are as sharp as ever.

"Tell me about Sister Nazarena, don Anselmo. When did you first meet her, and when did you become her confessor?"

Anselmo sighs. My question evokes many memories, including some unhappy ones, when Nazarena's voice through the curtained grate in her door gave him words of comfort that nobody else would give him. "In 1945 I was elected procurator general. A few days after arriving in Rome I went to see the Camaldolese nuns at Sant'Antonio. There were about twenty of them, in great misery."

"What do you mean, 'in great misery'?" I ask.

"Economic misery. The nuns said, 'Father Procurator, help us; we haven't anything to eat!' All they had to live on was the kitchen garden. Their only other income came from weaving the palms used for the Holy Week procession in the Vatican; it took five of them all year to do the work. As I got to know their situation, I started to ask questions. The nuns were confused and uncertain about their identity, and at the Vatican there was talk of closing the monastery. But my main contact, Monsignor Montini, the future Pope Paul VI, urged me to help them."

"Anselmo, about Nazarena...?"

"On my second visit to the nuns, she came to see me in the

parlor, wearing a long dress and a veil that covered her eyes. We exchanged a few words in French. She said, 'Please come again, Father, because there is a lot I want to tell you.' The next time we met, she told me about her family and her education—music at Yale, then English literature and French. With some hesitation she began telling me the story of her vocation. She had a vision: Jesus, wounded and weeping, appeared to her and said, 'I'm all alone—come stay with me!' Or words to that effect. She was overwhelmed by the experience, but she came out of it convinced that Jesus wanted her to live alone with him."

I ask the obvious question, "Did you believe her?"

"Wait, let me finish!" says don Anselmo. "When we met, Julia had spent eleven years trying to find a convent where she could live in solitude. Priests gave her no help. Her conviction was absolute, but no one believed her story of the vision, not even the papal deputy for the cloistered nuns in Rome, a Capuchin by the name of Padre Giovanni. After I started hearing her confessions, she wrote him to say she wanted me as her 'spiritual father' and would not speak to him any more. So he wrote the mother abbess, saying that he had always found her stubborn, willful, and totally undisciplined. The letter shows that he was incapable of recognizing a vocation that came directly from the Holy Spirit. She proved she had a call from the Spirit by coming to Italy, joining a small, impoverished community, and living an authentic life of prayer in absolute solitude."

"I have seen Padre Giovanni's letter, and it puzzles me that he called her 'undisciplined.' That she was stubborn I can agree; she had to have a certain toughness to face years of hearing priests tell her that the vision and the call to the desert were sheer illusion. But she could never have lived her life without being a very disciplined person."

"When he said 'undisciplined,'" Anselmo answers, "he

meant that she would not adapt her life to convent rules. That is why he didn't believe in her vocation."

"In other words, someone who can't observe the rules has no vocation?"

"No one believed there could be a religious life of any kind without 'regular observance,' that is, a life where everyone in the community follows the same set of rules. In those days no Catholic order besides the Camaldolese would let a religious live in total reclusion."

"Because they considered such a life to be 'singularity'?"

"No, because they considered it to be madness! But Nazarena never for a moment lost confidence. She kept humbly and calmly resisting the priests who judged her psychotic. In Rome she joined the Carmelites. After five years with them, the novitiate, simple vows, approval for solemn vows, she left the convent. She walked out onto the street without knowing where to go—what priest could ever understand her? But she was absolutely sure she was doing the right thing."

"The nuns of Sant'Antonio understood her and welcomed her into the community," I say. "After she had been with them for seven years, they wrote to the Holy See asking that she be dispensed from the canonical prerequisites and allowed to make solemn monastic vows."

Anselmo answers, "Even then, Padre Giovanni refused his permission. He called her 'a pathological case.' So I went to the Vatican to see my friend, Monsignor Montini, the future pope, and I told him, 'I have been hearing Nazarena's confessions since 1945, and I am convinced that during the last thousand years here in Rome no one has borne witness to Jesus Christ like this anchoress, who lives in solitude with a faithfulness and a generosity that go beyond every limit.'..."

"But there was something more than that." Anselmo lets me interrupt him. "Aside from this radical, stubborn consistency with her call to solitude, her personality was totally positive.

I've seen this in her letters: never a negative expression, never any of the complaints you hear from strict and austere individuals: 'The world is going from bad to worse, young people are selfish and rebellious, religious do not obey the rules any more....' Nazarena hardly ever used the word 'sin,' and then only referring to herself, never to others. You find her apologizing to the abbess, repenting of something she said or did, but never complaining about anyone else's faults."

Anselmo smiles. "You know what convinced me? The joy she radiated. Many times she said, 'Father, I am never alone. Jesus told me he would never leave me, and he has kept his promise.' She spoke about the 'Madonna' as if they were two little girls who sat and talked together. But this was not the essence of her experience. Nazarena's mysticism was her constant contact, her quasi-fusion with the Holy Trinity."

"This is essential," I agree. "Not visions of Jesus or Mary, but the life of the Trinity."

"Other visions she probably did not have; at least she never told me about them. Her greatest desire and her greatest joy were to participate in the passion of Jesus, for the sanctification of the church and the conversion of sinners. After years of struggling with priests and with her own uncertainty, she came to a deep sense of security and tranquillity."

"So you never doubted the authenticity of her vocation?"

"No, I never did, even though her vocation was exceptional in every respect. For me personally, knowing her was a great grace and a source of consolation. Fifty years ago, Thomas, you were just a child, while I was trying to reform the Camaldolese congregation. My only consolation was this anchoress; she knew my situation and my conscience better than I did."

"You could say that Nazarena was just as much your spiritual director as you were hers."

Anselmo nods his assent. "She perceived all my problems from within her silence and solitude. And she was always at peace—if you had only heard her! Her witness consisted in the peace, the joy, the tranquillity with which she lived her vocation. This was what convinced me."

Sister Nazarena and the Camaldolese Benedictines

Much has changed in our monasteries since the 1950s, and many of the changes for the better were initiated by don Anselmo, sometimes in the face of strong opposition. He was eventually vindicated by the general reforms in the church, at the time of Pope John XXIII and the Second Vatican Council. But Nazarena was always his closest confidante and supporter.

I ask him, "What advice did Sister Nazarena give you about reforming the Camaldolese?"

"It's hard to say," he answers. "I occasionally told my troubles to Nazarena, but she seemed to understand the situation better than I did. Sometimes she greeted me with a series of pointed questions, answered them herself, and said, 'Father, rest assured that it will all work out.' So I asked her, 'Who informed you about this?' She answered, 'Father, I could see and feel what you were going through.'" Anselmo pauses and sighs, and then continues. "I told her about the problems in our congregation and about my experience as a novice, and said, 'Nazarena, in spite of your authentic vocation you had to wait until you were nearly forty to start living the solitary life. We novices, at the age of fifteen, were told to stop studying and go live on bread and water in the hermitage. Do you see the contradiction?' Of course she did. 'You absolutely must change this situation!' she said emphatically. She had great inner freedom—it was as if she had been a novice mistress herself. In part she understood the situation from what I told her, but other things she grasped by reading my conscience. In any case, she supported what I was doing."

I have another question. "Did you encourage her to study? As an anchoress, did she read theology?"

"Yes," says Anselmo, "but she did not need my encouragement. She had an edition in French and Latin of the *Summa theologiae* of Saint Thomas Aquinas. She read all thirty-three volumes and acquired a deep grasp of Aquinas's thought. I complimented her on this, since I had used the same edition for my own studies. But she also read Scripture and the Church Fathers. Even while she was weaving the palms, for twelve hours a day, she kept the Bible open in front of her."

I am surprised. "Twelve hours? I thought she spent only two hours a day at manual labor."

"No, who told you that?" Anselmo replies. "She worked eight, ten, even twelve hours. Hundreds of palms had to be ready for the Vatican three days before Holy Week. I can't see how she did all that work, sitting in her tiny room. When I thought she might have a bit of free time, I asked her, 'Why don't you write something?' Once she wrote several dozen pages on monastic themes, at a time when we were revising the Camaldolese constitutions. She could have been a writer, had she not been totally engrossed in her intimate contact with the Lord, which she did not want to lose for a single instant."

Thomas Merton and Sister Nazarena

Don Anselmo tells me about his correspondence with Thomas Merton. "During the 1950s Merton wrote to me saying he wanted to become a Camaldolese hermit at whatever cost. So his abbot from the Trappist monastery in Kentucky came to plead with me not to accept him. But I said, 'What do you mean, telling me not to take him?' Then the abbot general of the Trappists came, and I said to him, 'Excuse me, do you have the right to tell me what to do? You think Merton is wrong to ask to become a Camaldolese hermit, and you may or may not be mistaken. But when he writes to me, how can you stop me from answering him?' In the end their will prevailed over his, and poor Merton wrote me saying, 'If I cannot

come to Camaldoli, you must bring Camaldoli to America.'
And so we went to California—this was when we founded New
Camaldoli."

I pause, remembering New Camaldoli as it was in 1961,
when I first went there. "What did Sister Nazarena think
about the American foundation? Did she offer you any suggestions? I suppose she was aware of your trip to America and
your plans for the foundation."

"Yes, she knew about it," answers don Anselmo. "She even
gave me a couple of addresses."

"And did she have hopes for vocations in America? Did she
think there were many people who would want to live as hermits?"

Anselmo hesitates, then says, "She was happy we were making the foundation, but you must realize that she had overcome all curiosity and ambition, and she never asked me
questions about the congregation."

"When monks from New Camaldoli started to arrive in
Italy and came to visit the nuns at Sant'Antonio, did Nazarena
notice it?"

"Of course she knew that some American Camaldolese
were here in Italy," replies Anselmo, "but I assure you, she
never asked about you. She was never curious about anything."

"That's all I wanted to know. She was not curious about us,
and yet when I went to offer mass for the nuns, I was aware
that she was listening. I felt that if anything in my sermon did
not seem right to her, she would not judge me, but would
only pray. Let me ask you something else. Did Nazarena ever
write anything in English?"

Anselmo replies, "She kept nothing in writing in her cell,
and she even destroyed all the letters she received, mine
included. She started writing me in French, and then in her
sort of 'Americanized Italian.' She wanted me to destroy all her
letters, but I didn't."

A Disciple of the Holy Spirit

"Nazarena's vocation was exceptional," I say. "She was convinced that no religious institute in the Catholic Church could have accepted the kind of life she felt called to, and yet the Camaldolese Benedictines in Rome took her in. At the end of her life Nazarena acknowledged that our congregation offered the natural environment for an anchoress. But tell me: How could she reconcile the canonical requirements of religious life with her conviction that she was called to live alone with God?"

"Because she was obedient," replies don Anselmo. "I felt she would always obey me." I start to say something else, but Anselmo continues. "Whenever I spoke of the Holy Hermitage of Camaldoli, Nazarena would ask me, 'Are there any empty cells there?' When I said yes, she would ask, 'Why can't you arrange for me to live there?' I would say, 'Nazarena, you can't expect me to do that—after all, we're in Tuscany, not in America!' After a few months she would try something else. 'Let me go to the Holy Land.' 'Yes, Nazarena, I would like to take you there. But if you want to live as an anchoress, someone has got to bring you a loaf of bread now and then, no? Who would do that for you—some Jewish people maybe?' And she would calm down again." Don Anselmo laughs softly. "She went beyond all laws, for laws only held her back. She would say, 'I feel I should do this or that...,' and I told her, 'All right, just put it in writing,' and I gave her my blessing. There was something stupendous about Nazarena's freedom, but I have heard people call it 'a grave defect.' Nazarena is an example of a heroic disciple of the Holy Spirit, who felt called to share fully in the passion of Jesus Christ. Unlike Padre Pio, she did not have the stigmata, and for this reason perhaps her suffering was greater."

"What impresses me about Sister Nazarena," I say, "is the absence of these paranormal phenomena. Aside from the 'blessed night' when Jesus called her to the desert, she had no visions, no stigmata, no miraculous abstinence from food. She ate and drank every day, even though it was mostly bread and water, and endured continual hunger pangs. She prayed, she worked long hours, and she lived by faith, hope, and love—this was enough for her and it should be enough for us."

Anselmo continues. "Her life was amazing in its simple consistency. Every night she got up at 1:30 and began her day of prayer, fasting, and work. She never doubted that this was what she should be doing. Once I asked her, 'Nazarena, would you like something different?' She said, 'Father, what do you mean?' 'I mean, would you like to take a break from being an anchoress and join in the community life for a while?' 'No, Father, that is not my calling.' And yet she was always free from structures and from her own rules. When you are a disciple of the Holy Spirit like her, the only thing you need is discernment. 'Whom did she obey?' The Holy Spirit. 'With what criterion?' With a confessor who tried to understand her and help her to discern. Period. 'What about laws and rules?' Of course, laws and rules serve a purpose, including the rules that govern our monasteries. For Nazarena the rule was her union with Jesus and the sharing in his passion—by fasting, by sleeping on a wooden cross, by remaining alone and hidden. She said, 'Father, I do not want to lose a single moment; every moment has to be an offering and a sharing in the passion of Jesus.'" Anselmo looks at me; his gaze is both gentle and intense. "Thomas, this is the only rule."

2. Correspondence with Augustin Mayer, O.S.B.

In 1947 Augustin Mayer exchanged several letters with Sister Nazarena. He was born at Altoetting in Bavaria on May 23, 1911. A week before his twentieth birthday he professed monastic vows at the Abbey of Metten. From the end of the Second World War until his election as abbot in 1966 he taught at the Benedictine theological faculty, the Anselmianum, a five-minute walk from Sant'Antonio. He also served as master of the student monks resident at the Anselmianum, assisted by an Italian Benedictine, Massimo d'Argenio, also mentioned in Nazarena's letters. In 1972 Father Mayer became a bishop, and in 1985 Pope John Paul II made him a cardinal.

A third priest from the Anselmianum remains without a name; he was the recipient of two important letters, in which, with great pastoral tact, Nazarena counseled him in a moment of vocational crisis.[1]

Cardinal Mayer told me very little about his personal contacts with the anchoress. Partly because of his advanced age and partly because of the reticence he learned through his many years of Vatican service, he volunteered nothing to satisfy my curiosity about Nazarena's personality at the time he knew her, when she was forty and had just begun her hidden life. But his eyes and his smile told me more than words could. From their first meeting he was convinced of her authenticity, and he trusted her advice in his own delicate task of forming future priests for Benedictine monasteries throughout the world.

Nazarena addressed some of her letters both to Father Mayer and to Father d'Argenio, saluting them as *fratellini,* "little brothers." They posed questions about fostering the contemplative spirit in their priestly ministries and academic careers; she responded with page after page of letters, notes, maxims, and finally with a grand, unsystematic "summary" of her doctrine. The following are only a few fragments, which present her favorite themes.

The Two Heavenly Teachers

Maestri celesti, she called the Holy Spirit and Mary, an expression that poses a problem of translation, as it contains a triple metaphor. *Maestro* is the "master of novices" in a monastery, the "teacher" in a school classroom, the "concert-master" in a symphony orchestra—hence, one who forms, teaches, conducts, "masters." Against the background of Father Augustin's professorship at the Anselmianum, the meaning of "teacher" prevailed, although the other meanings were implied.

> Nazarena wrote:
> God wants you to...focus upon yourself in order to liberate yourself from yourself and deliver yourself with perfect docility into the hands of the heavenly Teachers, the Holy Spirit and the Immaculate Virgin. It was they who formed the perfect Ideal of the Priest, Jesus Christ, and this is how all followers of the great High Priest are formed. The principal agents in the transformation of a priestly soul are the heavenly Teachers. The Sanctifier of souls, the Holy Spirit, does not operate independently of the Virgin, "in whose immaculate womb was formed the Christ."

> Priests who abandon themselves "blindly" to their guidance and protection, who let them have free course to act "in their own way," shall proceed not by giant steps, nor on eagles' wings, but at a divine pace toward perfection.
>
> If a priest is generous, docile, humble; if he withdraws and remains in silence so as to let himself "be worked over," without wishing to know, understand, or see the work they are doing in his soul; if he holds himself in quiet and silence, trusting them like a little child [Ps 131:2]; if he strives to silence the noise of the world, of creatures, and of the "ego," and if he strives to learn the divine art of listening to God's voice, the heavenly Teachers will not cease to work in his soul, and quite soon, as a result, in him will be formed the adorable image of the Christ.[2]

Nazarena gave first place to the contemplative dimension of ministry. Withdrawal into silence and into the listening heart is a necessary condition for outreach and effective work "with souls." Note the sense of the word *soul* as she used it: There is no Platonic dualism here; on the contrary, she employed the term—sometimes as common gender, most often with feminine pronouns—as a form of "inclusive language" before this became an issue in English theological discourse. "Soul" is the human person, insofar as she or he is capable of divinization, of transformation into Christ by the working of the "divine Teachers/Masters." The "soul" also has her own work, and it is the paradoxical "active passivity" of the mystics, that "striving" which translates into "surrender."

The Way of Surrender

The Italian word *abbandono,* like its French homonym, has become a technical term in contemplative literature; English translations often render the word "abandonment." Other terms, however, can be even more evocative: for example, "surrender," an expression of which Father Bede Griffiths was fond. Although the word implies the context of warfare, the military metaphor bears less weight than that of the lover's "surrendering" herself into the arms of her beloved. I find it best to alternate "abandonment" and "surrender" in translating Nazarena's *abbandono*.

Father Augustin, enthusiastic about Nazarena's spiritual doctrine, shared her letter with his colleague Father Massimo. They both requested further instruction. Father Augustin paid her a great compliment, to which she replied, "I must confess that your calling me an 'Apostle of the priests of Christ' inflamed my will truly to do all I can to become what you say I am! Yes, how much I desire to 'spur on the souls of priests'!" More and more freely she addressed their personal questions, but in doing so she revealed something of her own spiritual journey. Perhaps for this reason, she decided to cut off their correspondence after her profession of private vows in December 1947.

She saw Father Augustin's inner journey as paralleling her own. "I foresee sufferings and indescribable struggles, but I also foresee joys and moments of ineffable intimacy. These always go together: The greater are the sufferings, the struggles, the greater will be the joys and victories to follow.... When we are pierced with pain and the darkness is impenetrable, then we raise our pure and penetrating gaze. After the crucifixion, followed the glorious resurrection. Remember the words of Truth: 'Was it not necessary that the Christ should suffer before entering into His glory?' [Lk 24:26]."[3]

Sometimes Nazarena spoke of the spiritual struggle in military-athletic terms, but she preferred the unheroic "little way," inspired by Saint Thérèse of Lisieux. "Make small but constant efforts to overcome yourself in all things," she wrote, "hoping for victory in heaven, in the Lord, in Mary Immaculate; quickly and confidently get back on your feet after every fall, and start walking again with greater élan, with all the holy joy of a child who is sure he is loved all the same, in spite of his little falls. The heavenly Teachers are full of mercy and love, always ready to help and forgive and believe you when you promise, 'I'll do better next time.'" The way of spiritual childhood is possible only for those who surrender to unconditional love. "Cast far from your heart and mind the false and depressing concept that the heavenly Teachers are harsh, demanding, intransigent, that they turn their back on you the moment you make a false step!"[4]

Nazarena willingly mixed her metaphors. "Ah, be generous and courageous! May the divine offensive you have undertaken with such élan become a continuous and joyful advance. Plan well the little nothings you offer to the heavenly Teachers; do not undertake too much, be humble, never have pretensions beyond your strength—on the contrary, these nothings must be offered with great delicacy and tact, prepared with great faithfulness and constancy, accompanied by a sweet song." Here Nazarena echoed the Benedictine doctrine of *discretio*—discretion and discernment, the humble awareness of one's own limitations, as the primary criterion in spiritual practice. The ultimate criterion, of course, is love: "Love, accompanied by the proof of love—joyful sacrifice!"[5]

The mark of those who surrender, who abandon themselves to the divine work of mercy and love, is joy. "A spirit of deep, deep faith...penetrates through absolutely everything until it sees the mark of God's work: joy, holy and constant joy even amidst tears (if there are any)—'again I say to you: rejoice' [Phil 4:4]."[6]

Through the exercise of abandonment, the spiritual life is greatly simplified. Those who practice it surrender the right to dwell on past failures or worry over future fears.[7] "It is impossible that God will let fall from his arms a soul who surrenders herself to him with pure, blind, and loving abandonment to him alone, to his omnipotence, to his love, to his mercy. He permits us to fall when we believe we are able to walk on our own and we leave his embrace—he does not cast us away, he only allows us to walk off on our own so that we may convince ourselves that without God we can do absolutely nothing." Few are those who have this awareness of being carried in God's arms, and that is why our religious practice is so unmindful and mechanical.[8] Priests betray this lack of awareness and abandonment when they vest for mass and celebrate the liturgy in a slovenly and careless manner, reciting the prayers like parrots.[9]

A synonym of "abandonment" is "self-forgetfulness." "Unless you forget yourself totally," Nazarena told Father Augustin, "God will be unable to take total possession of you. God reigns sovereign only in those hearts which have been disencumbered of all that is not God." The unencumbered heart is the place of silence, where the "divine Guests"—the Father, the Word, and the Holy Spirit—abide. "As soon as you realize that you have allowed your attention to stray from the divine Guests, bring it back; but do so calmly and gently—never with impatience or violence. Never be discouraged. If you do nothing but continually bring back your gaze after it has strayed, the divine Guests will be content with your constant efforts in the midst of your falls."[10] Again and again, Nazarena returned to this: "Never yield to discouragement, agitation, anxiety."[11] The way of surrender requires above all great patience with oneself, which alone leads to total self-forgetfulness.

Mary, Mediator of the Mystical Union

When counseling Augustin Mayer and others, Sister Nazarena insisted on ardent devotion to the Mother of Jesus. Her Marian devotion had a special character to it, which removed it from the realm of sentimental piety and placed it within the eschatological horizons of her existence as an anchoress. Nazarena drew her understanding of the Blessed

Virgin from the few biblical references to her and from the dogmas of the Catholic Church. Mary is the Immaculate Virgin, assumed body and soul into heaven, the Mother of God and mediator of Christ's earthly existence and heavenly grace. Only rarely in her letters do we find the title "co-redemptress." In all of Nazarena's approximately five hundred letters, not once did she refer to any of the famous apparitions of the Virgin—neither to Lourdes nor Fatima nor Medjugorje. Nazarena no longer relied on her own "visions"; much less did she rely on those of others.

The ministry of priests, of "other Christs," wrote Sister Nazarena, must have Mary at its center. No sermon should lack at least the mention of her name.[12] Constant reference to the humanity of Jesus and Mary is a necessary remedy for an erudite theology that tends to shrivel up into abstraction. "Scholarly apparatus" is an ironic expression that Nazarena employed, not in the usual sense of annotations to a text—footnotes and manuscript references—but as a metaphorical title for priests and professors whose repetitive theology suffocates the affective breath of the faith and whose academic ambitions infect them with the many vices of the proud.[13] "God has no regard for great works and resounding success," wrote Nazarena, nor for theologians "who preach their own glory and not his—these machines, lifeless and sterile, incapable of infusing a single spark of divine ardor into the hearts of their listeners, for the 'scholarly apparatus' are nothing but miserable machines devoid of divine life. They speak from themselves, relying on the 'apparatus' and not on God; they speak in vain,...without any divine vision."[14]

For Nazarena, the liturgical linking of Mary to the Bible's personified Wisdom suggested what theology should be: a truly "gnostic" understanding whose fruit is prayer, love, and mystical union. Nazarena invited her "brother priests" to kneel at the feet of the Mother of the one High Priest and pray "that she will make you understand what great weight of merciful love is wrapped up in the word 'priest.'" She exhorted them "to close your eyes to all that you experience in the world and open them in sacred silence to the divine world, to welcome the infusion of this divine experience that uncovers bit by bit the unspeakable wonders of God and the sublime greatness of the priesthood, to listen to the divine voice which will sweetly tell you what you must do to become less and less unworthy of the priestly character."[15] The true priest is one who follows Christ, the divine model of priesthood, to Mount Calvary and to the shedding of living drops of love until no more is left to shed.

Nazarena lamented the cold-heartedness of many priests. "How much one senses, in the majority of priests, the lack of intimate union with the divine Victim! What glacial chill! They celebrate the most sacred mystery with only a surface awareness of the great work that is to be accomplished through their ministry." The remedy for the coldness, superficiality, and mediocrity that render even sacred actions a waste of time is to have frequent and fervent recourse to Mary, the Throne of Wisdom: "There from its wellspring you will draw the divine science that will transform each and every moment into a precious treasure for God and for souls."[16]

Devotion to Mary, according to Nazarena, is not an end in itself. "The humble Handmaid of the Lord, who keeps nothing for herself, will in the silence of God lead the little child to Christ. And Christ receives with love and tenderness all those whom his beloved Mother gives him.... Everything begins and depends from Mary. Where are those who hold their heads high and think they can do without the humble Handmaid of the Most High God? Look around you, and see if you can find intimate union with God in a single soul who is not devoted to Mary! Look again—see if you can find an *alter Christus,* a true 'other Christ' without devotion to her who is the inseparable companion of the One par excellence who forms the 'other

Christs'"—that is, the Holy Spirit. In other words, if a priest's formation and life do not replicate the ontogenesis of the Incarnate Word in Mary's womb, Christ will not recognize him as his brother and his other self.[17]

Again it is abandonment, surrender, that makes it all simple. "My dear little brothers, how truly simple is the spiritual life, the divine journey: abandonment deprived of sight yet full of love and confidence in the Immaculate Virgin. She will do all the rest! All the rest with the Holy Spirit, with the Christ, with the Blessed Trinity!"[18] Mary herself is the model of the blind yet loving surrender to God. When Mary chanted her Magnificat, "for an instant she transcended herself—she focused on God's greatness, and her soul, leaping for joy in the All of God and the nothing of herself, immediately made the canticle resound for God's glory, not for her own, and her thanks went to the Giver."[19]

Christ welcomes the soul clothed in qualities proper to Mary, yet shared by all who "do the will of the Father in heaven" and who thus become his "mother" (Mt 12:50). "With what love he embraces her and draws her to his heart, 'in which all the jewels of wisdom and knowledge are hidden' [Col 2:3], and there, resting on his heart, the soul penetrates the mysteries hidden from the wise and prudent of this world [Mt 11:25; 1 Cor 2:6–8], hidden from the scholarly apparatus, hidden from those who rely on the excellence and the virtues they presume to possess, hidden from those who want to enter into great intimacy with the Master, Christ, without following the way the Most High showed us: the immaculate way of the *Tota Pulchra*," the "All-Beautiful" Mary. She is the "gate of heaven," but she is also the "lowly handmaid"; whosoever would enter therein must bend down. The soul who does so discovers that God, the Holy Trinity, likewise bends down to her.[20]

Reading the "Divine Code"

A recurrent metaphor in the maxims of Nazarena was "God's code," the cryptic message of love in everyday realities that we, by putting on "God-glasses" (*occhiali divini*), can decipher. "Abandonment is really nothing but living each moment...with, through, and in the divine world that dwells within. It means holding steady your gaze, your thoughts, and your whole self in intimate contact with this divine world." The person who discovers this inner world begins and concludes every thought, word, and deed therein; even when one is asleep, one's center is there, "and when you wake, you continue joyfully and lovingly to live under God's gaze, breathing God's atmosphere."[21] "Every moment, with its joy and its pain, bears the mark of God, which is immediately recognized by the soul who is accustomed to read the 'divine code' in every message, every word, every event."[22]

Whatever the circumstances, what counts in God's eyes is not our success or failure, but our intention; if we see as God does—that is, if we wear "God-glasses"—we will not be troubled or anxious about the quality and quantity of our actions; our only concern will be the spirit with which we perform them. Nazarena saw the expression "God-glasses" as a good synonym for "the spirit of faith." If we wear them throughout the day, "the littlest things we perceive or read or see or hear will lift us up to the world whence all comes—the divine world. The same thing applies to all events, vicissitudes, wanderings, joys, sorrows, etcetera. Everything is a message, an envoy, a breath, a breeze of the divine world." [23]

The word *breeze* reminded Nazarena of a biblical image dear to her, often evoked during the years in Carmel: that of Elijah at the mouth of the cave, who hears God not in the earthquake nor in the tempest, but in the "still, small voice" of a gentle breeze (I Kgs 19:12). Deciphering the "divine code" in things small as well as great "gives a supernatural tint to our

whole existence; it makes us live in an atmosphere totally per-
meated with the divine." The consequence is not alienation
from reality. "At the same time it keeps us united to this world,
it makes us act 'divinely' in everything, for everything, with
everything.... Nothing is excluded, however banal or of little
material or spiritual value."[24]

Nazarena felt that Father Augustin was already close to the
mystical awareness of God's message encoded in life itself.
"Accustom yourself to look upon absolutely everything with
God-glasses; if you do so, you will live in a divine atmosphere,
and everything will be transformed into God." When you have
learned to move and act on God's plane, she told him, breathing the divine atmosphere, "you will live with your body on
earth but with your spirit on high, far from all creatures; all the
things of this earthly exile will cease to exercise the same
power, domination, and influence upon you, and their tyranny
will be broken."[25] But again Nazarena hastened to remind him
that mystical consciousness is not a state of distraction from
everyday tasks. On the contrary, it heightens one's awareness
of the value of "little things." "Our whole life is woven of these
little, everyday things, and if the tapestry is lacking in beauty,
what is the outcome? It is because we believe that we have no
need of God in the banal matters of every day, and we do not
take the trouble to ask God to help us with them. 'After all, I do
them every day, they count for nothing,' etcetera.... What is 'of
little importance' for the divine world, where every act has a
weight both divine and eternal?"[26]

The "little way" is grounded in the Gospel (Mk 10:15) and
in Saint Paul's doctrine of salvation by grace through faith.
There are not a great many citations of Paul in Nazarena's letters, but one often hears echoes of 2 Corinthians 12, Galatians
5, and Philippians 4. Like the Apostle, she "boasts of her
weakness"; abandonment to God means seeing in oneself no
virtue, but only God's gifts, and of these none can boast. The

following letter to Father Augustin is dense with these Pauline themes.

> The soul who thinks only of the glory of God and not of her own is made to penetrate deeper and deeper into the unfathomable abyss of God's Majesty. God will grant her clearer and clearer glimpses of some of the rays of divine splendor and entrance into the holy place of the One who alone is holy. There, mute before the marvels of the divine beauty, in profound adoration, from her enchantment she will pour forth the "Holy, Holy, Holy" in divine silence....
>
> God communicates intimately only with those who recognize and love their own nothingness, and they, the more deeply they dig into the bottomless abyss of their nullity, glorify the All of God.... The better we know our nothingness, the greater will be our capacity to receive the wondrous largesse of God's goodness....
>
> Far be it from us to associate God with words like *hard, strict, tough, miserly, intransigent;* to say it like this seems absurd, but if we examine ourselves closely, we will see that in practice our attitudes toward God and the way we relate to God do not glorify the infinitude of God's attributes and perfections. Blessed is the soul who contemplates God through this word *infinite,* who...tunes her voice to an *infinite* pitch and sings the ineffable, inconceivable, incomprehensible glory of every divine attribute and perfection.
>
> Yes, brother, the deeper we plunge with joy into the depths of our own nothingness, the more God will send down to us eminent graces, and these will lift us up to the divine heights.[27]

3. Counseling the Camaldolese

Once again, don Anselmo is our best source for a more precise understanding of Nazarena's sense of belonging to the monastic order of Camaldoli, a feeling that was strong enough at times to draw her out of her habitual hiddenness and to make her express interest and concern—always felt, but normally expressed only in prayer—for her sisters and brothers in religion.

In 1954, addressing the mid-term chapter of the Camaldolese Benedictines, don Anselmo proposed a wide-ranging constitutional reform of the congregation. He and others had made the proposal a decade earlier, and questionnaires had even been circulated. This time their motivation was strengthened by the desire to found a community in the United States. Again, the move toward the Americas was not new; the monk-hermits of Tuscany had begun and then closed a flourishing foundation in Brazil (1899–1926), while the Camaldolese monks of Saint Michael were in Bryant, Texas, from the 1920s until their suppression in 1935. Consequently, don Anselmo wanted to draft the new constitutions in view of the projected American foundation.

Although the Camaldolese nuns have their own customs and constitutions, they have always been closely coordinated with those of the monks. Don Anselmo kept Mother Ildegarde informed of his projects and sought her advice. Nazarena, always in favor of closer ties between the male and female branches of the order, felt called on to make her own contribution. We have a series of typewritten documents, rambling essays on monastic life, that the anchoress addressed both to the abbess and to don Anselmo. The fact that she typed them indicates her desire that they be preserved and even examined in the commission charged with revising the constitutions. Of course, she was also thinking of the American foundation as she wrote.

> Be sure to pray to Our Lady, in whose spotless hands the Lord has placed all the graces he wills to grant us. May she obtain for you the grace to prepare the new articles of the constitution "according to God," as he wills it. The one thing necessary for everyone, everywhere, at all times, and in all circumstances is the holy will of God. It is our one and only rule....
>
> Do all you can to make the liturgical Hours the only obligatory vocal prayer for everyone.... When the student monks [from San Gregorio] come here for Vespers, they sing so well! I am so very glad to hear them. When the monks preach retreats, it would be good for the retreatants to hear some Gregorian Chant—the devout chanting of monks could do so much good for souls! It makes a deep impression on them, perhaps deeper than a lot of other things....
>
> The religious orders that want to be exclusively solitary condemn a part of their membership to live the [active] life of Martha. Who could survive, if everyone wanted always to live in solitude?...
>
> Doesn't it seem that the best (if not the only) solution is to organize the order so that those called to live the cenobitical life are an integral part of it? Thus a monastic who has no call whatever to live as

a hermit need not think he or she has not fulfilled the monastic vocation, remaining always a cenobite. As things are now, the Camaldolese cenobite is considered practically a "midget." Who, with a clear call to community and not to the hermit life, would want to join the Camaldolese and be considered a "spiritual midget"? The cenobitical vocations all go—obviously!—to the other Benedictines or to the Trappists, where they can find their "respectable" and "honorable" place. It is also obvious that good and holy cenobites could offer immense help and support in an order where there are solitaries....

If the solitary life were maintained at the highest level, accessible only to those favored by God with a free and evident gift, it is obvious that there would be very few solitaries. But if so, the monastics who belong to the larger number would not feel so "ashamed" that they are not one of the privileged few. They would live their divine calling with holy peace, joy, and thankfulness, without feeling they haven't "arrived." They would not need to feel they were lacking in generosity or had failed to respond to God's call.[28]

Nazarena's radicalism was paradoxical. On the one hand, she wanted solitaries to be truly such, and not, as she warned, "a mockery of the solitary life," as happens when those called to the common life of the monastery are forced to live in the hermitage.[29] On the other hand, she insisted that it was natural that authentic solitaries be few in number, and that the majority of the Camaldolese live in community and not as hermits. It was clear to Nazarena that this typically Camaldolese pluralism, with hermitages and monasteries, solitaries and cenobites, all belonging to the same monastic family, must be codified precisely in the constitutions. She wanted the Camaldolese to have a "precise and distinct physiognomy," which Saint Romuald himself failed to provide. "Camaldoli's misfortune has been precisely the abuse (you could almost say) of its admirable liberty of spirit and broadmindedness. Details are lacking. Too much is left undefined! Too much—much too much—freedom is left to the superiors!" This has led to "arbitrary, individualistic interpretations," which in turn have given rise to dissension and division in the order.[30] Nazarena summed up her vision of the Camaldolese Congregation:

> Camaldoli must not present itself as a purely eremitical order but rather as a contemplative order which is able to receive, form, and develop to the full every sort of contemplative vocation, from the cenobitic to the anchoritic....
>
> The specialization of Camaldoli must be contemplation. We must have absolutely nothing more to do with running schools or hospitals, etc. (Leave such activities to those who are specifically called to engage in them.) We must no longer waste personnel and talents getting ourselves entangled in any kind of active service except that of retreats.
>
> With regard to the nuns' constitutions: Since they have not yet been submitted to the Holy See, don't you think they should be completely reworked? Shouldn't we write completely new constitutions, adapting them to allow for hermitesses and anchoresses? We could introduce into our constitutions what the monks did not succeed in introducing into theirs....
>
> When you write about Camaldoli, you ought to emphasize that an integral and honorable place will be given to the cenobites (if they had only done this

from the start...). Authentic eremitical vocations will always be relatively few. No hermit order will ever expand, if it does not embrace within its bosom the cenobites as well, giving them, as I said, their rightful place.[31]

Today, most monks and nuns of our congregation have forgotten—or have never known—the polemical aura that once surrounded the words *hermit* and *cenobite*. Paradoxical in view of Camaldolese history and spirituality, this polemic is understandable in the light of changing ecclesiological paradigms. Following the division between Eastern and Western Christendom, and with an increasingly "juridical"—as opposed to "Eucharistic"—ecclesiology prevailing in the Latin Church, monasticism as such found itself pushed more and more into a narrow niche, whose boundaries were defined exclusively in terms of "observances," with reference to generic "religious life" wedged between clergy and laity. Monasteries of men, originally lay communities (Saint Benedict was a layman!), became "clerical institutes" on a par with modern orders and congregations, while nuns were treated as little more than "women's auxiliaries," often reduced to the status of "domestic servants."

The Camaldolese—born as a monastic order of men and women (sometimes united in joint communities), of cenobites and hermits, of anchorites and missionaries, with options of lifestyle that ranged from parish ministry to perpetual reclusion—simply had no place in the Catholic Church. Ill at ease with juridical categories—we are not simply "religious" (much less "clerical"), nor can our life be defined as a series of "observances"—the survivors at Camaldoli could take refuge only in pure conservatism. Since hermit life was "characteristic" of Camaldoli at its origin, the Hermits of Tuscany could only live as the "opposite" of cenobites, whether the Camaldolese of Saint Michael or the Trappists or the "Black Benedictines." The riches of early Benedictine and pre-Benedictine monasticism were no longer a shared heritage, and the terms *hermit* and *cenobite* were reduced to buzzwords.

In Nazarena we find nothing of this polemic. She intuitively grasped the deepest sense of Saint Romuald's personal charism and of the original spirit of Camaldoli, and she reaffirmed the unity of the monastic vocation in the plurality of its forms.

If we think back to those days, perhaps we can arrive at a compassionate understanding both of don Anselmo and of his adversaries, whether hermits or Vatican functionaries. In 1957, back from the United States, Anselmo found himself the object of grave accusations, public and anonymous, on the part of a few monks at Camaldoli.[32] He sought Nazarena's counsel and comfort, and while she did try to console him, she called his attention to the spiritual opportunity his suffering offered.[33] In one of her letters, after a prayer to Jesus, she added a series of maxims, addressing Anselmo as it were in Jesus' name: "There are souls who rank high in the eyes of worldly people, but there are many others who, hidden in humble occupations, are just as useful workers. Moved as they are by love, they are able to change the least of their actions into spiritual gold, by immersing them in my blood.... When a soul is cold and disheartened, everything seems hard and painful. Let her come and rest in my heart [Mt 11:29]. Let her offer me her discouragement and she can be certain that a day lived thus will be of incalculable value for souls. My heart knows all human miseries and feels infinite compassion for them."[34]

To no one did Sister Nazarena ever recommend the use of the hair shirt or other corporeal penances. As an extreme remedy for his wounded pride, she did recommend them to don Anselmo.

4. Letters to Metilde

A young nun of Sant'Antonio, Sister Metilde, later to be mistress of novices at the Camaldolese foundation in Africa, posed a series of questions to Nazarena. One day, accompanying the anchoress to a dentist's appointment, she had the rare opportunity of conversing with her. "For a while I was providing the materials for Sister Nazarena's work," Metilde reminisced, "and once I even taught her a new way of weaving the palms. I turned to her for spiritual counseling a few times, at a difficult moment in my life. It was in 1967, and as we were on our way to the dentist together I started asking her questions. Hearing me say that I had lost my sight in one eye, Nazarena said to me: 'Ask for a miracle!' And I said to her: 'Sister Nazarena, you ask for the miracle; if you have faith great enough for both of us, the Lord might grant it to me.' She also told me a doctor had advised her to get her cataracts operated on. Nazarena struggled over this, because first she decided to do it, yielding to the will of God, but when it was time to go to the hospital, she didn't want to leave her reclusion. Mother Abbess didn't know what to do. The doctor assured her he would keep her in the hospital no more than one night; only then did she consent to the operation.

"She also helped me in my duties as assistant novice mistress. I had accepted this office with a certain repugnance and a bit of fear. After Sister Nazarena had written to me a few times, Reverend Mother said to me, 'Metilde, what have you done?' 'What do you mean?' I asked. Mother said, 'Why did you trouble Sister Nazarena?' Nazarena, after she had spoken with someone, was often troubled in conscience and wouldn't leave Reverend Mother in peace. And so Mother Abbess said, 'It's all right, you can keep these letters for now; later, bring them to me.' Nazarena kept asking me to tear up the letters, and so I made lots of little tears around the edges and told her I had torn them, and then I put them in a folder and took them to Mother Abbess."[35]

The salutation of the first two letters was formal: *Cara Donna Metilde*–"Dear Dame Metilde," but the third opened with only the name, and later Nazarena would greet her simply as *sorellina,* "little sister"–a crescendo of familiarity, echoed in the content of the letters.

> Remain at peace and thank Jesus, because he is the one who lays his hand on your soul [Ps 139:9], in order to purify and detach you from all that is not himself, and to prepare you to receive the immense gift of loving union–provided you let Jesus do it and accept whatever suffering you have to undergo, as he brings the divine work to completion. You must not want to understand anything. Surrender yourself to him with all generosity and courage. Let him do whatever he wants, without offering any resistance, without desiring or seeking any consolation. For the soul it is a terrible suffering, to let God destroy all that is not God. Few are those who allow God to perform this very painful operation, and thus there are few who reach the heights!
>
> Aim at fulfilling your duty in all things, with great faithfulness, and be glad if it costs you to do so and if you feel no consolation while doing it. This is an exercise in pure love and will make you

proceed with giant steps. The soul will be ever stronger and more generous, if she is faithful....

Do not be discouraged if all you see is your own misery and weakness, and if you experience more and more your incapacity, impotence, and the like. This will be necessary, in order that the soul may empty herself of all self-esteem and cast herself for all and for ever into God's arms.[36]

Nazarena used similar expressions in her correspondence with Father Augustin Mayer, twenty years earlier. But as the two sisters gained confidence one with the other, the anchoress advanced into subtler themes of ascetical and mystical theology, revealing the depth of her personal experience. Although she never held the office of novice mistress, Nazarena showed profound insight into the ways of monastic initiation, guided by the classical Benedictine principle of discretio—"discernment" and "discretion," a wise and humble sense of one's own and others' limitations.

Since those who have just begun the novitiate do not possess solid virtue but have to acquire it, it seems to me that the best thing to do is not to come down hard on their defects at the start. They are still weak and frail—being hard on them will do more harm than good: It would strike them down and leave them defeated and discouraged.

Instead, it would promise better results if you work on their good qualities and virtues in order to reinforce them, thus infusing trust and courage into the novices. Then they will start struggling with their defects bit by bit, beginning not with those which are dominant and have the deepest roots in human nature—these are the most tenacious and the hardest to overcome—but with those defects which yield more easily. Small victories with minor

defects will give them the courage and trust necessary for the war against defects which are harder to
uproot. Regarding these, we must never lose heart
nor stop struggling, just because we continually fall
and are defeated by them. Emphasize that what
counts is to keep struggling, with trust, calm, and
joy, never letting oneself succumb to defeat, even
when one continues to fall.[37]

Positive reinforcement, not severity, is the most effective
way of correcting faults. Nazarena counseled Metilde to
"remember what Jesus said about the wicked servant who
called his master 'a hard man' [Mt 25:24]. He was judged
severely according to the severe judgment he had of his master."[38] Later, Nazarena would apologize to Metilde for being
too "severe" herself: "With severity nothing good is accomplished."[39]

A typical fault of novices is a kind of perfectionism and
impatience that expects all persons and circumstances in the
monastery to favor one's own spiritual progress. To purify the
novice of this vice, said Nazarena, "God permits that there be
at least one thing or one person like a thorn in the flesh [2 Cor
12:7] which keeps [the monastery] from being 'heaven on
earth.'... Becoming agitated, complaining, or trying to get rid
of it does nothing but aggravate the pain."[40] This wise counsel
assumes even greater weight in the light of Nazarena's profes-
sional training in music. Perfectionism is the occupational
disease of classical musicians, and Julia carried this vice with
her even when she became the anchoress Nazarena. But rarely
did she project her passion for perfection outside herself. She
would blame herself for every infraction of her scrupulously
detailed rules, every unnecessarily long conversation, nearly
every letter of spiritual direction she wrote, but never did she
blame the community of Sant'Antonio for not facilitating her
practice of "silence and solitude."

Patience is strength, in the person charged with forming others. "When you see the novices are resisting you, avoid correcting them or pointing out their faults. When difficulties arise, the novices are restless, and their passions are aroused, then tell them frankly, 'Now is not the time to resolve this problem. Let us wait and pray over it.' After the initial impact, their passions will quiet down, and they will see the problem more clearly. Recourse to prayer brings light, grace, and strength. With all this, you are quite ready to resolve the problem in a holy and profitable manner. Otherwise, if you deal with them while the fire is still burning and you haven't full control of yourself, you run the great risk of throwing oil on the flames. In the face of problems and conflicts, if only we knew how to wait, in silence and in prayer, until things calm down again!"[41]

Nazarena reminded Metilde that she was not the teacher of the novices; they were being formed directly by God. "You are to speak and act in the name of Jesus and for his sake. To do so is possible only by remaining united to him; otherwise, instead of speaking and acting for his sake, you will speak and act in your own name. When dealing with the novices, you ought to keep one eye on the Holy Spirit and with a glance ask: 'What must I say to this novice? How should I answer this other novice? What must I do in this mess, when problems of this sort arise?' Then you must be silent and listen attentively to God's inspirations—the voice of the Holy Spirit, the Inner Guide, the only One who knows the path that each soul must tread. If you do this and stay where you belong in God's relations with the novices—as the gentlest instrument of the Holy Spirit, in order with docility to convey to them God's voice, will, warnings, and corrections, which are both firm and gentle [Wis 8:1]—then you will see more than ever how it is the Spirit, the Divine Teacher, and not yourself, who is forming the novices and sending them on the way to holiness with generous, loving, joyful, and docile hearts."[42]

Nazarena herself practiced this gentle approach in spiritual formation. The anchoress was aware that her "little sister" was looking for a word of comfort,[43] and she balanced her words carefully between exhortation and consolation.

> As soon as I read your second note, I felt I had to help you find the right direction on the dark and painful path where God has placed you. I want you to stay on this path and journey to the end with great faithfulness, generosity, courage, and love — this is the way of radical purification and absolute detachment from all that is not God alone—the preparation for the supreme grace, the transformation of your soul in love. This demands the death of the ego; it means giving absolutely everything in order to receive everything from God, our poor nothing in exchange for the All, which is God. No price is too great for this divine gift. Be ready and happy to pay it, refusing nothing to the Lord, who wants your whole being so as to give the divine Being wholly to you.
>
> So I am thinking of writing you a long letter, and I shall try to let the Holy Spirit, the Spirit of love, the Spirit of Jesus, the One who sanctifies souls,...use me as a docile pen, so that I can write down a few things for you, in the hope that they will give you light, comfort, encouragement, and so forth. You can read them bit by bit, choose those few things which may be of help to you, and leave aside the rest.[44]

The Dark Night

Sister Nazarena suggested that Metilde read *The Dark Night of the Soul* by Saint John of the Cross. In her letters she elaborated some themes of the Carmelite doctor, but without attempting to corroborate what she said with direct citations of his writings. Nazarena was speaking from her own experience, and while using the metaphor of the "dark night," she gave it an original interpretation. She was sure that Metilde would understand this teaching, since, in her opinion, the young nun had already entered into the first stages of the mystical "night."

> [The dark night] is a great, divine gift, because it means that God's own hand now rests upon you [Ps 139:5] in order to prepare you, bit by bit, to ascend to loving union with God, provided you do not set up obstacles and force God to stop working in your soul. So rest assured about "that suffering" you are undergoing. Thank the Lord for it.
>
> The dark night is a new state. In it we experience things we never felt before. We do not understand. The soul feels lost. Darkness, aridity, impotence, and the like cause great pain. One must not want to understand or to see anything. Suffer everything in holy peace and with great trust, in spite of the fact that God seems to have abandoned the soul. God is closer than ever, caring for the soul with a very special care! Because God is infusing a strong and pure light into her, the soul sees defects and imperfections which previously she could not see, while she was in the dark. Do not be surprised when you see yourself more imperfect than ever. Do not think Jesus has abandoned you....
>
> You need to concentrate on seeing and feeling that without God's grace you are more and more lowly, weak, and incapable of the least good. This places the soul in the pure truth. Only a great and pure light — God's own gift—can make the soul see her nothingness, weakness, misery. This is an incalculable help in

emptying the soul of all self-esteem and self-confidence, so that she will throw herself into God's arms
and put her hope for every least good in God alone.
In this way she glorifies God's mercy, goodness,
power, and love. It makes the soul come out of herself, come away from self-reliance and self-concern,
and look to, and count on, God alone....

Give greatest attention—always!—to charity and
humility. The lack of these keeps us from God and
God's grace. Acts of these virtues attract God to us
and draw down grace upon us. Immediately and
fully forgive every least offense and never dwell on
them again, and Jesus will do the same with all your
offenses to him! Think of this, always! Be a great
soul, who quickly rises above all human miseries,
not a narrow, gossipy soul, who wastes and loses
time and grace over the least human misery. How
much attention we must—always!—pay to this! How
easy it is to waste your whole life, your vocation,
and God's grace with human miseries and the vani-
ties of this passing world!

With these thoughts I leave you now, my dear
little sister, in the arms of God, the Holy Spirit, in
the Heart of Jesus, under the mantle of the heavenly
Mother—love and pray to our Lady, take shelter in
her in moments of pain and difficulty! If you do so,
what grace and help she will obtain for you!...
Upward and onward, always![45]

The anchoress's letter answered many of Metilde's questions but raised still others. The young nun felt intimidated by
Nazarena's high ideal and lofty, mystical doctrine, and so she
wrote again. Nazarena immediately sent Metilde a short note,
promising a fuller explanation. "It seems strange to me that
you wrote that note and that I answered it—but—I think Jesus

was behind it all, because he wanted you to have a little word of encouragement from someone who understands the state you're in, since she has experienced it herself. It is a state rich with great hopes, if you remain strong, steadfast, and if you let Jesus make you bloom into a divine reality. Remember these words of Jesus: 'Abide in my love' [Jn 15:9]."[46]

Within a few days, Metilde received several closely written pages, a little *summa* of Nazarena's doctrine.[47] The anchoress's point of departure was a phrase in Metilde's letter that complained of her "many acts of unfaithfulness that make one lose heart." Nazarena repeated the advice she had given the abbess years ago: Discouragement is more spiritually harmful than any of our imperfections or faults, since "it comes from the devil and from our defeated self-love." Human weakness and succumbing to surprise temptations are occasions for renewed confidence in the Lord. "This sort of unfaithfulness," said Nazarena, "does not offend Jesus at all."

> I even think it gives him pleasure to see a soul run to him not with head held high for its successes, but with head bowed and contrite heart, full of trust in his love and mercy, sure of his forgiveness. For Jesus it is a joy to grant his divine pardon to a heart full of repentance and love....
>
> When souls have made their decision to give their all to Jesus and are making generous efforts to give their all, they think they will soon become saints; they do not realize they are behaving as if everything depended on themselves. Then, when in spite of their generous efforts they do nothing but stumble on the path, maybe even more than they used to, they lose heart. It is a surprise for them! They don't understand!

The Lord, said Nazarena, "permits repeated failures and unfaithfulness," in order to convince us of the words of the

Gospel: "Without me you can do nothing" [Jn 15:5]. When we cease to be surprised at our imperfections and failings, this is a first sign that we are making progress; when at last we overcome self-pity and are even glad when we behold our imperfection, "these are signs which conceal no illusions."

In the background of Nazarena's teaching on spiritual progress was the metaphor of the "ladder," especially in its Benedictine formulation, "The Degrees of Humility," from chapter seven of the Rule. However, Nazarena's approach was original, because she saw the opposite of humility not in pride, but in "that blind and thoughtless self-confidence and self-reliance which block the free flow of grace." Note that "self-confidence and self-reliance" are two pseudo-virtues strongly inculcated in American schoolchildren; Nazarena's understanding of them as obstacles to the "flee flow of grace" expressed her opposition to the counterfeit morality of America's secularized Puritanism. At the same time, said Nazarena, the readiness to repent of our failures helps us find in them "a new occasion to glorify the mercy and love of Jesus, which are infinite and limitless."

> Without grace it is impossible to do the least bit of good. God bestows grace upon the humble and denies it to the proud [Jas 4:6; Prv 3:34; Ps 138:6]. To move forward, and even more to climb to the heights, how much humility we need! How much grace of God we need! Hence the soul who wants to receive an abundance of grace must study herself in order to profit from everything that reinforces this necessary virtue—humility—in her.
>
> To be honored and praised, to enjoy great success, far from being means to obtain humility, are for the most part a great hindrance, if the soul desires them, if she seeks them, if she takes pleasure in them. If only the ambitious, vain, and proud souls

knew what harm they are doing themselves! They
are blocking the grace of God! Not for nothing the
saints fled honors and positions of rank, and went
forth with joy to meet humiliations, contempt, all
that is low and despised. They were in the Light.
They walked in the Light [Jn 8:12, 12:35]. God
rained down upon them the abundance of his
graces of predilection, because they were empty ves-
sels, capable of receiving God's divine rain of grace.

Metilde expressed fear and even repugnance on being
assigned the office of assistant novice mistress. Nazarena
encouraged her, indicating both the pedagogical method and
the inner attitude a monastic should have in assuming such a
responsibility.

Yes, your office is quite difficult, even one of the
most difficult. But since it is, in no way can you rely
on your weak and inept nature. So place the full
weight of the office on the shoulders of Jesus—then
stay closely united to him. So good and so strong is
Jesus, that he will bear not only the burden but you
yourself; however, you must keep closely united to
him and leave the whole weight on his shoulders....
Any office which involves responsibility for
souls, far from being an obstacle to union with
God, obliged as you are to interact so much with
souls, the office is and must be a great means to the
most intimate, close, and continuous union, since
you must speak and act for God. This is possible
only if the person who represents Jesus stays
closely united to him; otherwise she is speaking
and acting in her own name, whence follow who
knows how many human miseries.
Give of yourself to the novices to the extent that
your office requires, without counting the cost. The

more you sacrifice yourself for them, the more Jesus himself will be at work in your soul, taking care of everything for you. This will be of great profit for you. "Whoever loses her soul for me will find it!" [Mt 10:39]. If you flee from duty, you flee from Jesus and from his grace, and you will find nothing but yourself!

Nazarena's spirituality was radically eschatological; her ascetical doctrine was radically Christocentric. Jesus is the model of self-sacrifice, but he is also the object of our gift and the agent working within us, enabling our generous giving.

Jesus has given you the gift of a generous heart, capable of loving much and of sacrificing yourself for those whom you love. So now, do all you can to exploit to the maximum this divine gift. See Jesus in everything and everyone, especially in whatever causes you pain, see the occasion to give him a great gift, "to give rather than to receive" [Acts 20:35], to follow him with a generous and loving heart on the way of the cross, that he may continue in you and with you his great work of redemption. Do your utmost to lose sight of yourself, to think no more about yourself, to lose yourself in God, letting God do to you and with you whatever he wants. The Peace of Jesus, that holy Peace which tastes of eternity, can reign in the soul only when the noise of the ego and all its racket are eliminated. To the extent that you are dealing with the ego, to that extent you will not be dealing with God. If God does not take things in hand, the soul by herself will never succeed in dealing the ego the deathblow, so that from its ashes may arise the new creature, all purified, all transformed.

Passive purification, the "dark night," the "deathblow to the ego," albeit painful, are signs of divine predilection. "Jesus loves you so much," said Nazarena, "more than you can imagine." This love, and grace itself, are not "cheap"; the gifts expected from us are costly. However, the cost of them must not become an obsession for us, for anxiety about the cost will only block our generosity.

> So as not to lose courage nor to waste time thinking about sacrifices to come (which maybe will never come!), you need to work at acquiring the habit of living with all your might only in the present moment, putting into it—for this is what counts and is decisive—all the love you have. Jesus bestows his grace only for the present moment. He does not give me now the grace for tomorrow, not even for an hour from now. If tomorrow he asks me to make a costly sacrifice, he will give me grace to do it at the moment I am to do it, provided that, instead of getting upset and troubled about the sacrifice, I do not focus on the sacrifice, which would only weaken me, but on him, putting forth my hand to receive from him the strength and courage which I do not have. If I cling to his grace, I shall overcome. I shall do what, of myself, I cannot do. "By the grace of God, I am what I am," says Saint Paul [1 Cor 15:10], whose life was a continual sacrifice crowned by martyrdom.

> What weakens you and makes you lose courage in the face of the cross is focusing on the cost of the sacrifice and then looking at your own weakness—then and there, all your strength is gone. If you do things this way, all is lost before you begin, of course!

> But let me repeat, because it is so important: In the face of the cross, do not focus on the cross, but learn

how to look deep inside that wood, with a gaze of faith and love, and find hidden there...Jesus, and with him the grace and strength to bear, with him, for him, and for souls, the weight of that cross. And think of the holy peace and joy which will follow, because you did not turn your back on Jesus and his cross: no remorse of conscience, no troubled thoughts or sadness or loss of grace for your own and others' souls. You need to let these things sink deep into your soul, so that after a while you will not need to reason things out so much in order to gird yourself with courage, but the instant the cross appears, love will rise up immediately. With joy and élan go forth to meet Jesus; open your arms and embrace the holy cross with and for love, and faithfully follow him to the mount of joyous self-immolation.

Love plays the leading role. Love is the great motive for living. Love, and Love alone, lets you bear the cross with joy and faithfulness and makes its burden light and easy [Mt 11:30]. Only Love has the medicine, one drop of which in a cup filled with bitterness can transform that bitterness into sweetness. What power has ardent Love! Love made the martyrs go forth fearlessly and with joy to meet their martyrdom. Love allows God to slowly nail the ego to the cross, until he strikes the deathblow that lets Love reign sovereign, who in turn consigns the kingdom to Love Supreme, who is God [1 Cor 15:28].

Jesus has to listen to such noisy complaints and protests as soon as he draws near with his cross; so for him it is a great joy when he finds a soul coming out to meet him with love songs, whenever he and his cross are near. What ravishes him is the song of pure love, which sounds most beautiful when he extinguishes the last glimmer of light in the soul's firmament, leaving her in thick darkness and depriving her of the least drop of consolation. Upon the soul who sings him that song—the purest and loveliest of them all—he bestows the great, divine gift, that one drop of the divine tonic which, in her cup brim-full of bitterness, contains such force and divine energy, that without her realizing it she starts climbing the steep path in darkness with giant steps, all unawares, thanks to that divine tonic. At the top of the mountain of pure love he stands.

Realizing that the many pages she had written might be too much for Metilde to take in all at once, Nazarena apologized and concluded with a chain of biblical quotations.

Ask our Lady for the grace and strength, so that "he who has begun a good work in you may bring it to completion" [Phil 1:6]...without your impeding him or forcing him to stop completing that great, divine work—the greatest of them all. Learn to keep your soul in holy peace and quiet in the midst of darkness and trials, suffering all that God wills and for as long as he wills, resting your soul [Ps 62:2] in total self-surrender to him, in self-giving with no thought but to give rather than to receive [Acts 20:35]. Do all this, moment by moment, fully sanctifying the divine moment, clinging to the grace of Jesus, hidden in him in that "moment by moment." The more you hide yourself there, the more you must believe that he is standing closer than ever, strengthening you, helping you climb, without your realizing it. For the love of Jesus and of souls, throw yourself totally into the "good fight" of which Saint Paul speaks [2 Tm 4:7] and let the grace of Jesus win the final victory, bit by bit.[48]

A Gentler Way

Metilde grasped Nazarena's essential message, but many nuances escaped her. In years to come, with the complete loss of her eyesight, Metilde herself would acquire wisdom through experience, and become a spiritual mother to the nuns in Tanzania. But in 1967, not yet tempered by her African experience, she felt unready for the dark night of the soul. So in a brief note she questioned Nazarena and asked whether there might not be a gentler way to union with God, a way not of the night and its passive purifications, but of spiritual sweetness, to woo the soul from her attachments and fears into the divine embrace. Metilde asked Nazarena to pray that this might be so. The anchoress replied, in a tone of surprising severity:

> You want me to pray that Jesus will give you "much sweetness"? Far be it for me to pray for such a thing, because if you are fed only sweets, you will always remain a baby soul. Both with and for Jesus, I wish you were a full-grown, generous, and robust soul. You "have so great a need" for much sweetness? You're wrong! You have a great need of hard, dry bread, because this—and not sweets!—is what makes souls strong, generous, courageous. You want to be generous and strong; you want very much to love Jesus. Jesus sees this. So in order to make you what you want to be, he is beginning now to feed you with the bread of strong and generous souls. He wants you to love him with a pure intention, for his sake alone, not for the sweetness of his gifts. You will never reach your goal if he has to give you "much sweetness" now.
>
> Don't you see that what you are seeking is not Jesus but the consolations of Jesus? You are seeking yourself, your own enjoyment, your own consolation

rather than that of Jesus. Hence from now on you must do your best and give your all for a total and complete detachment from yourself, from everything, even from the consolations of Jesus. Instead of thinking of yourself, of how much it costs—dryness, desolation, sacrifice—think of the countless, eternal fruits contained within the generous and joyful acceptance of painful dryness, desolation, sacrifice, and so forth. Think of the joy and consolation of Jesus, when he sees you endure and love what causes your suffering, so that you give him the sweets and keep the hard, dry bread for yourself.[49]

Think of yourself closing the gates to eternal torments and opening them to the eternal bliss of heaven, for the sake of so many souls who would not be saved, were they not helped by the prayers and sacrifices of their brothers and sisters in Christ. Oh, do open your heart and your mind to the eternal value of each moment! Take advantage of every moment, for Jesus and for souls....

Be ready for many years (maybe) of fasting on nothing but hard, dry bread, without a drop of consolation. You will never reach total detachment by eating sweets, but only by many long years of fasting. How hard it is, how rough and steep the climb to the top, to total detachment, but what a great thing you find up there! God, the highest Good, the supreme Beauty, and in God, everything and everyone. Only to the totally detached soul can God grant the abundance of consolations, because such a soul is not attached to God's consolations but to God alone. So you see, if you really want "much sweetness," you will have to pay a very high price for it: long years of painful dryness, of being abandoned by God, of absence of consolation, of trials and sacrifices. Now that Jesus is giving you the coin to pay the divine price for the "much sweetness" you desire, oh, be ready to thank him for his gift to you! Pay the high price with holy joy, while at the same time you are earning so much grace for so many souls, so that one happy day they also may enjoy the sweetness of Jesus....

Learn to keep a great, divine silence in the temple of your soul and listen attentively—maybe the Teacher of teachers will grant you the gift of hearing the voice of God's inspirations. In a single moment God can make you understand more than the lessons of a thousand teachers.[50]

We do not have Metilde's reply to the letter. Perhaps she explained that the "sweetness" she desired was not so much for herself as for the novices, so that in their simplicity and spiritual immaturity, they might not be frightened away by so arduous a challenge as that which Nazarena had placed before her "little sister." Whatever Metilde wrote in reply, it evoked from the anchoress an apology and a further clarification.

I was really glad to receive the last thing you wrote, because I was pained at the thought that I might have been too severe, and that I might have hurt you instead of helping you, because with severity nothing good is accomplished. So I was glad to know that you understood my note in the spirit with which I wrote it, and also to know that I had given a wrong interpretation to the "sweetness" you wrote me about....

It is sweet indeed to feel yourself loved, but should Jesus one day want you to undergo the terrible feeling that he has forsaken you [Ps 22:1] and that you have no one to rely on, be strong, generous, trusting, and in spite of everything believe that Jesus is closer than ever. I do not know what the future has in store for you. There is no need to lose time thinking about it; just be prepared and ready to accept whatever may happen. I say this, because my wish for you, as I have just said, and my hope, is that you will never let yourself lose heart or take fright at any trial or adversity....

To bear fruit, we must do everything in "the will of God"; outside of this, not even martyrdom suffered for the sake of a soul would have any value [1 Cor 13:3]. I am so glad to hear you speak of God's will and to see you so well disposed to accept it, whatever it may be—this is everything! Hang on to this and be faithful, and you can be sure never to go wrong. However, you must not trust your own judgment but submit everything to one who speaks to you in the name of God; if you do this, you will be walking by the safest and holiest route....

We need to know ourselves well, both the good and the evil in us. But we must spend only the minimum amount of time necessary to reach this self-knowledge, so as not to waste precious time worrying about ourselves and analyzing ourselves continually. Most of our time should be given to God and souls. Ego is the hardest obstacle to overcome. The supreme victory is when you overcome yourself. Happy the one who wins this victory!

You told me not to worry about these letters of mine, but you didn't say you tore them up, as I asked you several times.

I am asking my little sister to imitate her big sister in one thing only: Your big sister tears up every letter she receives. Sometimes she even tears them up without reading them, if they were letters she wanted very much to read. The more she wanted to keep a letter, the more she forced herself to tear it up. She only keeps letters from Jesus, written in no language but that of God. Do the same yourself, like your sister. Make her happy and tear up everything she wrote, including this.

I do not speak in the name of God but only as your sister. Take my sisterly advice for what it's worth and only if it fits you. Forget all the rest.

And now, dear sister, I must leave you. I leave you with tranquillity and confidence in the arms of Jesus, because he loves you and will love you always, so very much, and because I see that you return his love. Love casts out fear [1 Jn 4:18]. It includes everything. It will never fail [1 Cor 13:8]. May the divine Teacher tell you all the many other things, which I have not said. Listen to the Holy Spirit with docility and love.[51]

5. The Voice of Sister Nazarena

Few people heard the anchoress speak. Don Anselmo knew her voice well, having listened to her confessions and shared their long conversations over more than four decades. Mother Ildegarde exchanged words with her regularly, sometimes at length. And yet many nuns lived with Nazarena for all the forty-five years she was at Sant'Antonio and never once heard her voice. One who did (a nun who wishes that I do not use her name) conveyed to me the substance of a conversation she had with the anchoress.

The nun knocks on Nazarena's door, and Nazarena pulls aside the curtain that covers the grate in the door. "Good morning, Sister Nazarena," the nun says.

Nazarena replies, with a very soft voice, "Good morning."

They exchange a few words regarding work. Then the nun asks, "How are you feeling, Sister Nazarena?"

The anchoress replies, "Oh, not well. I don't ever feel well, Sister."

"No? Why not?"

"This is what I wanted here, to suffer greatly. I accept it quite willingly. It's what makes my life fruitful. Maybe it could help others, or Jesus could make it a help for others. So in spite of everything, I don't think about myself. You see, when you love God, and souls as well, you suffer willingly. It is like a joy, a consolation, if you think it will help others. It is so hard for us to understand hell, but if you suffer so that no soul will go there, your suffering is a consolation, and you willingly accept it. Even if it means you never sleep any more and the pain is very great and almost endless."

The nun starts to say something, but Nazarena continues to speak. "Oh, Sister, how many failings I have—what blindness! And what a failing it is, when even consecrated souls strive to be appreciated by others, to have a good reputation. Even many priests in the active apostolate, however hard they work, make this mistake. While if you trust in God and are convinced that you count for less than nothing, God's gaze rests on your soul. This conviction of my own nothingness helps me so much to be detached from everything."

"How?"

"For me, the thought of humility, of not wanting to count for anything in this world, and the thought that God looks on the world and takes pleasure in one's soul—this is a great consolation. It helps me to be free from attachments and to follow this path faithfully. But one who tries to do good to others and at the same time to be successful so as to enjoy their esteem—this is wrong, it is harmful to the soul. Of course it isn't a grave sin, but what help is it for others, if we are sinning like this all our life? We get poorer and poorer. We either advance in virtue or in the lack of it. People think that, whatever happens, it is possible to take a step forward and then a step backward, so as to stay in the same place. No, Sister: In every moment it's either forward or backward, depending on the intensity with which we perform every action. And remember: Every little thing has its value." Nazarena exclaims, softly, "But then, what peace!"

The nun interrupts the anchoress. "Nazarena, you once promised to write down a few thoughts for me."

"Oh no, I must not do any writing. I must not write anything except what is strictly necessary, because my vocation is not to move out toward the world, but to go into the desert."

She insists. "Don't you remember, one day we talked about

this? I asked you to write down a few thoughts for me personally. Because I don't live in reclusion. I live in a community and come into contact with many things. So I need someone to support me."

Hesitantly, Nazarena replies, "Yes, don Anselmo told me, under obedience, that I must write. As long as it was something only the Spirit was telling me to do, I put obedience ahead of what I felt. My self-will needs someone who speaks with authority and who doesn't have anything to do with what I feel or want. I do something only when others can observe in me that I absolutely would not act without obeying. You see, there is something that has to come before writing, even when it is the Holy Spirit who is telling me to write. I had to be really at peace about it, since I still have other work to do. And so I must do this first, before I start writing. I have to do one thing at a time, and then I can be at peace. I hope the Lord will bless what I write, for you and for me, and for those who will read it, because I'm doing it as a great sacrifice, against my own will."

"But then it's God's will..."

"Yes, that's what I'm counting on. I hope God will give me the grace. But you get grace in no other way—only when the Holy Spirit gives you light. I have to recognize, too, how blind I have been up to now. Because the more light the Spirit gives you, the more you see your own blindness. I pray the Spirit will enlighten us, starting with the others. Do you understand? The more you see the Holy Spirit enlightening others, the more you see your own blindness. And then the Spirit reveals what is objectively real, and you begin to see better." Nazarena is silent for a moment. "And Sister, whatever I write will be for you, personally. I don't want anyone else to see it, because I'm doing it only for you."

The nun reassures her: "Oh yes. No one will ever see anything. As long as you live, it will remain in your room. But do write down everything, all the details about your life."

"Sister, when I write I have to write spontaneously. I put on paper whatever comes to my mind. I'm not complicated..."

"That's it. The Lord will enlighten you. If you need another notebook, I'll bring you one."

"No, I have several notebooks. Now I have something more to tell you. I am glad that you see the first, the only thing really necessary for the spiritual life. The one thing that has to do with God is desire, because if God is always your desire, the Lord will bless you always. I feel you know this, and I'm glad to see that you desire to go forward. So be consistent with this, dear Sister. We are what we desire, that is, the desires that come from us; as are our desires, so are we. The more you strive to have a pure intention, the more the Lord blesses you and gives you light. Try to be faithfully consistent...it isn't easy, but neither is it complicated."

"That's it, straight and simple."

"Straight and simple. You need to be very mindful, even of one wrong and uncharitable desire. By grace be mindful of the Lord." Nazarena changes the subject and says a few words about an alarm clock that needs repair. Then she says, "Sister, this is the last time you should come. I want to begin living my life, which is that of an anchoress. My only desire is to dedicate myself to the one thing necessary. This is the last time."

"What do you mean, 'the last time'?"

"This is the last time I will let myself speak about these things, beyond what is necessary. Because I mustn't speak to others, except to my spiritual father and maybe with Mother Abbess or a superior who has to decide something, but only about necessary things."

"So, you will not even speak with me. O.K., provided you write!"

Nazarena says, "I hope I didn't make you waste your time."

"No, of course you didn't."

"But Sister, do try to seek the one thing necessary."

PART THREE
A Silent Prophecy

1. Questions about Nazarena

Nazarena conceived the life of an anchoress in apocalyptic terms. She projected each moment she lived in the cell—the prayer, the work, the frugal meals of bread and little else, the writing of letters to her abbess, her confessor, and others—into the end time. In a sense there was no history for Nazarena, because she lived her personal history, together with the history of that corner of Rome visible from her open window, at the point where time crosses over into eternity.

She was not obsessed with demons or other denizens of hell, even though they afflicted her sorely; her *eschaton* was the heaven of God, of Jesus and Mary, of the angels and a few saints dear to her. When Nazarena imagined herself as an angel of mercy, using Christ's chalice of blood like a key to shut hell's doors and open heaven's to souls at risk, her Apocalypse became Eucharist. This was her vision of the end; her mission in time was to tip the scales in favor of heaven, of salvation, of eternal beatitude. Had she known the Russian saints, like the blessed starets Silouan of Mount Athos, she might have prayed for a final harrowing of hell, in hopes of the apocatastasis of the damned.

The eschatological projection of her life demanded that she remain hidden. Hiddenness, for Nazarena, was more important than solitude. Her mission was to preach a paradoxical sermon that would reach the world only if it remained unheard. Her life was a silent prophecy of the end, of the eternal glory to which God has destined every creature.

Reading her letters, you are overwhelmed by the power of her conviction and the depth of experience from which they well up. As you read, you find it impossible to suspend judgment—whether you share Nazarena's experience or not, whether you believe as much as she does, she makes you share her joy. But after the reading, you set the letters aside, and questions come.

In the letters to Metilde and to Cardinal Mayer, you see how Nazarena's sense of time present was compressed into the end time. Even though her mindfulness of the here and now and her following of the "little way" kept her radical vision of the end focused on God's incarnation in time, she gives you the impression of not belonging to this or any other age. The letters to Metilde leave hardly a clue that they were written in the 1960s, during the restless times after the Second Vatican Council. The good Pope John XXIII and his sometimes hesitant successor Paul VI led Roman Catholics once and for all out of the mentality of fortress and ghetto into an adventurous and uncharted voyage on the seas of dialogue with other faiths, and into a clearer sense of belonging to these modern and postmodern times. By contrast, Nazarena's mystical doctrine seems immobile; it could fit into almost any century, from the fourteenth onward.

Now and then, however, she gave a hint that she knew where and when she was living. One day in 1986, after mass, Sister Ilda, bringing holy Communion to Nazarena, found a note that the anchoress had pushed out under her door. It said: "Please do me the kindness of knocking when you come this morning. I wish to ask you a question."

Ilda knocked. The curtain behind the door rustled and Nazarena spoke: "What has happened to *my America?*" She had heard a prayer during mass; one of the nuns had remembered the astronauts who were killed in the explosion of the

Challenger space shuttle. Ilda, being a very patriotic Italian, was struck by the fact that this woman, out of touch with all news and away from her country for some fifty years, could still identify with "her America" and feel concern for a tragedy that shook American public opinion like no other space or military accident.

Still, the Nazarena you meet in her letters was a woman out of time. She had nothing to say about grave events going on around her, like Fascism and war. Fifty years later, her silence seems almost to mock the evil of them, like the levity of Groucho Marx entertaining the troops in Europe just after D-day. Sitting in the field tent of an army general, Groucho heard the radio telephone ring. He went over, picked it up, and in a cheery voice said, "Good morning. This is the Second World War. May I help you?"

Obsessed with her "calling," with her search for the desert, she seems to imply that the war and its aftermath were somebody else's business, not hers. Arriving in Fascist Italy, Julia shopped around for a convent that would let her do her own thing—seek Jesus in mystical prayer and penance—without joining in a real community life.

This is a gross caricature, of course, and the implicit judgment is wrong. It is true that Sister Nazarena did not speak of evils like Fascism and the Holocaust and atomic war, and the reader may think that she lived as if they never happened. But can you conclude that she was silent about them because she had no heart for her fellow humans who were being oppressed and gassed and bombed? This has to be wrong, because it fits neither her personality nor her circumstances during the forty-five years she spent in reclusion.

If you regarded massive human suffering as one banal news item among many, if you could answer the telephone and say "The Second World War"—like Groucho—with the same tone of voice as an operator who says "Sear's Mail Order Service," then you could not spend almost half a century in a small, bare room eating nothing but bread and water and sleeping only three hours a night—like Nazarena—and still be a sane, affectionate human being, as she was. The person she became at the end of her life revealed the sense of what she set out to do after her vision of the suffering Savior in 1934. "In my end is my beginning."

Still, you could question Nazarena. You might admit that her life in reclusion was somehow "the will of God" for her, but you could still ask whether it has relevance for anyone but herself and a few cloistered nuns and Camaldolese hermits. You might answer your own question by saying that she fell prey to an illusion but simply had the kind of robust physical and psychological constitution that could survive and even thrive under a skin thickened and hardened by privation and discomfort.

But you would face a dilemma. Nazarena was more suspicious of illusions and self-deception than were any of her superiors or confessors. She repeatedly insisted that no one in the convent, especially the younger nuns, was to imitate her reclusion and her penances. She felt all the discomforts to which she subjected herself, and as she grew older, she became more and more sensitive to the cold weather, the monotonous diet, and the rest of her austerities. She started, perhaps, as a tough lass, enthusiastic for hardship, trained in sports and in the perfectionist discipline of classical piano and violin. But at the end of her life, Sister Nazarena was a sensitive and ailing senior who tried her best, without succeeding perfectly, not to complain about aches and pains and the winter chill. Many questions, it seems, remain unanswered.

However, a clue to their answer is found in the undertone of all her letters: joy. She did what she did because she was "following her bliss" (as Joseph Campbell might have said). Pleasure and pain were both transparent to her; she saw through them to the love that "endures all things," and so she did not choose pain over pleasure but rather love in everything.

Was love an abstraction for Nazarena? Did she love only a series of mental projections: "Jesus and souls"? Many of the nuns I interviewed had, on rare occasions, come upon Nazarena in the hallway (she would leave her room and go to the monastery library while her Sisters were at table or asleep). They remember how she greeted them, with a silent bear hug and a couple of warm kisses. They have no doubt she loved them in a very personal and concrete way.

At the beginning of 1977, after more than thirty-one years of reclusion, the anchoress felt the need to defend, not so much her own person, as the grace the Lord had given her. "My life does seem—yes!—sterile, wasted, egotistical, etcetera, in human eyes, which see only outward appearances (and indeed I appear quite full of defects). But in the eyes of God, who sees my desires and my little, persevering efforts to do what I do with faithful, generous, and trusting love, who knows?—maybe my poor, hidden life, as sterile and wasted as it appears, has opened and is opening the gates to eternity for many souls who have lived their lives in mortal sin. Precisely because I know that everything I do is defective and deserves to be rejected, I give it value and a divine quality by uniting it, through lively faith, limitless hope, and ardent love, with the Sacrifice of the Redeemer."[1]

Nazarena was aware not only of her fellow monastics but also of people outside the monastery. Her window was always open (to avoid turning on a light); it looked out over a one-way street called Clivo dei Publícii. She did not stand at the window, lest someone see her, but she could hear the happy voices of children just out of school, the soft voices of some young couple out walking in the long summer evening, the excited gossip of the American college students, guests of the nuns, on their way to visit a museum or a church or a Roman monument.

Nazarena's dream of the wilderness of Judah came true in her simple, bare cell in the Camaldolese monastery of Sant'Antonio. Although Nazarena's letters are full of the rhetoric of the desert, of an absolute, rigorous solitude, her rhetoric reveals its true meaning when you see the room she chose to live in and the monastic house the room belonged to, with a large window open all day, looking out on a city street and on the ruins of a Rome that once had an empire.

The trees and a wall across the street somewhat restricted her view, but she could see the ruins on the Palatine Hill, and after the war, on the slope below the monastery, she saw roses being planted in what was once a Jewish cemetery. She did not speak of what she saw, but the view was there, and it entered into her prayer. When she died, the nuns said, her eyes remained fixed on the window, in the direction of the rose garden.

Nazarena's solitude posits a distinction between "relevance" and "meaning." Solitude embraced as a space for contemplative prayer is deliberately irrelevant. The choice of solitude, if it is not hypocritical, implies the will to remain hidden and unknown. How can I be relevant to people who do not even know what I am doing?

Thomas Merton was, for many, a "relevant hermit," in spite of his insistence on the necessary irrelevancy of all contemplative forms of life. But Merton was anything but hidden. From the time he made his solemn monastic vows in a busy Trappist abbey among the Kentucky knobs, he let the world know, through a best-selling autobiography in the style of a novel and its many sequels, that although he was enjoying his "elected silence" in the monastery, he would rather be alone on some mountain (maybe at Camaldoli in the Apennines), still writing books about it. There is no question that Merton was rich in relevance, but was his life richer in meaning than Nazarena's?

Relevance is a transient quality. A book, a liturgy, or a political movement is relevant because it is up-to-date; time passes, and it is dated. Meaning is for all seasons. Merton, the relevant hermit, is hopelessly dated, at least in his language, because

1968, the year of his untimely (irrelevant but, I think, meaningful) death, preceded the linguistic revolution that started to make the English tongue gender-inclusive. "Man" and "men," for the human person and humankind, now sound wrong when we read them in Merton. In a way, the outdated "Jesus and souls" language of Nazarena is refreshing: We enjoy the frequency of feminine pronouns, since the word *soul* is feminine in Italian, and if she speaks of Jesus, we certainly do not mind the pronouns "he" and "his," while we do mind them when God is always "he," and the seekers of God are almost always "men."

Of course, I have not answered my own or anyone else's questions about Nazarena. I have, however, begun to find a deep meaning in her letters, a meaning that speaks to me, personally, not only as a monastic but also as a human being and a musician living out the last years of a horribly violent century. Sister Nazarena—together with another "eschatological" and hidden saint of our time, Silouan of Mount Athos, whom I have already compared to her—consoles me in my irrelevance, and teaches me the positive, even redemptive meaning my lesser contemplative calling can have, in relation to the victims of twentieth-century violence.

2. Story and Theology

The story of Nazarena, as of any Christian who lives a divine vocation to the full, is a theological source, a *locus theologicus* within Holy Tradition, because Tradition itself is chiefly story. A theology that grows out of Holy Tradition is narrative theology. Ancient Christian writers did not elaborate theological systems apart from story. Monastics did their *lectio divina* on the whole narrative heritage of synagogue and church, and they made no radical distinction between the stories of Abraham and Moses and the lives of Saint Antony or Saint Benedict.

Modern revivals of *lectio* tend to isolate biblical Scripture from the whole body of Jewish and Christian writing. The easy availability of small, one-volume Bibles favors this. But Saint Benedict, in Chapter 73 of the Rule, puts the Old and New Testaments on the same footing with the Lives of the Desert Elders, at least as far as monks are concerned. A Psalm, a page from the Gospel, or the story of a holy monk or nun is "a norm of human life." Nazarena read the Bible but understood it within her own, lived experience. In a very real way she became the verses she read and quoted. When we look at her life and her letters, we are reading a translation of holy Scripture.

Nazarena chose to live her vocation within a religious institute, but she did not need institutional approval to follow God's call. It would have been no less clear to her, had she continued to be repulsed by priests and religious superiors, as was the case for eleven years from the time of her vision.

However, you do not see in Nazarena simply an American individualist, a libertarian, go-it-alone, do-it-yourself maverick. Nazarena demanded that the church recognize her call in terms of the church's faith, whatever the church's laws and institutions could make of it. If anything, her mission was to oblige the twentieth-century church to accept an out-of-time religious reality that in other eras—premedieval and medieval—had been present in Christendom, even though it could be in communion only with a church that did not yet have a code of canon law.

A recent essay on medieval anchoresses and anchorites gives us an insight into their place in the precode church.

> On the one hand, [anchoritism or reclusion] was an alternative religious vocation: the laywoman chose it in lieu of the monastery. On the other hand, it was an advanced form of monastic life: the nun took, beyond her original vow, a new and irrevocable step to greater austerity and an intensified spiritual life.... Men and women lived both as anchorites and hermits in the twelfth century. The two ways of life were well defined and distinct from each other. The twelfth-century Englishwoman who desired a religious life had three choices: she could become a nun, an anchoress, or a hermitess. To choose to be a nun or an anchoress was to have a fairly sure notion of what that experience might entail. To become a hermitess was to enter into a much less charted land, one so unclearly drawn for women that no name for them quite existed. Both men and women are *anachoretae;* they are *inclusi, inclusae, reclusi, reclusae.* But women are not styled *heremitae* in biographies and chronicles. We call them 'her-

mitesses' because they are women living the equiva-
lent of a hermit's life, but they are not so named in
the texts.[2]

The anomalous and archaic character of the Camaldolese
Benedictines enabled them to fit Nazarena into their canonical structures and hence into those of Roman Catholic religious life. The Carmelites had no place in their institutional
structures for someone like Nazarena. Their reform was cenobitical and rigidly enclosed, in the case of Teresa of Ávila's
nuns, austere but not purely contemplative, in the case of the
friars. But even the nuns of Sant'Antonio were unable to keep
Julia the first time she joined their community.

Reading Sister Nazarena's letters, we see she was no Teresa
of Ávila. Nazarena told us part of her story, but while doing so
she veiled the psychological dimension. There were only a few
dreams, but no real self-analysis. She saw a vision once, and
no more.

Nazarena was also unlike Hildegard of Bingen, because she
was too liberal to share the ideas of that twelfth-century German aristocrat. For instance, she did not share Saint Hildegard's idea that a woman is a weak creature who has
something to say only if she is a visionary. Nazarena was not a
visionary, and she had nothing to say that was not already said
by her life. Chastity was not an important theme in Nazarena;
it was almost an obsession for Saint Hildegard. Music was
there, but Nazarena threw away all her compositions, including one loyal attempt to write a mass in Italian. Her genius was
too great for her talent, and it could be expressed only in her
life, not in her art.

She owed much to Saint John of the Cross, but freely differed
with him on a number of points. She took his "Cautions" to
heart, and she lived the "dark nights" of which he wrote, but she
had a different and richer experience of them than what is suggested in *The Ascent of Mount Carmel*. She owed much more to

twentieth-century America than to sixteenth-century Spain or twelfth-century Germany.

The closest Nazarena came to quoting John of the Cross's doctrine directly was in one of her letters to Sister Metilde.[3] Other expressions of Nazarena that seemingly alluded to John of the Cross were simply common ascetical-mystical doctrine; she may have found them in textbooks of ascetical theology or even in monastic literature, for example Jean Leclercq's summary of Gregory the Great's mystical doctrine:

> [The soul] is drawn to [God] by contemplation, in a naked prayer full of light; for contemplative prayer is a contact with a splendour so far above [the human], that in order to reach it [one] must be free from everything that is not the divine light, and attain to a simplicity and poverty of spirit which reflects and participates in its infinite purity. In an act of adoration and humility, of love and self-forgetfulness, a soul feels something of this purity: she knows it in not knowing it; for if she had some knowledge of it she would not realize that it is utterly unknowable. [Pope Gregory's] asceticism is governed by this theocentrism: contemplating God, the soul feels the nothingness and defilement of anything to which she still clings which is not God; she wishes to disengage herself, so as to remain in the presence of God with nothing in her which would be an obstacle to the light. She wishes to forget and, as it were, 'to sleep to all other things.' More and more, grace takes possession of her, and she perceives that gradually the power of grace breaks all her attachments to creatures. God and [the human creature] are Saint Gregory's two contrasting poles, and they are brought together by salvation through Christ in the Holy Spirit.[4]

The theological principle established by Pope Gregory and later invoked by John of the Cross is that none of the human faculties (not even the intellect or the will) is capable of receiving God, and so union with God is had only by direct God-soul contact. This contact is known by the one who is so touched, but the soul cannot describe it to herself; hence the faculties are at a loss and end up suspended, as the divine union takes over the soul's energies. John of the Cross called this suspension a "dark night"; other metaphors could do as well.

You might say that Nazarena was like Thomas Merton, who kept telling the world he wanted to live the kind of life Nazarena was living. The difference between them is that he never got to live a true anchoritic life, and for this reason he remained always a bit frustrated. Merton needed the frustration as a goad for his art; Nazarena needed no goad. Nazarena did what Merton talked about, while talking very little about it. From another point of view you could see Nazarena as the anti-Merton, the opposite of the eremitical rhetorician.

In *Raids on the Unspeakable,* especially the chapter entitled "Rain and the Rhinoceros," Thomas Merton says a great deal about solitude and the Christian hermit (and about the Zen person) that I find it easy to disagree with. Merton is against having fun; Merton is for the "free man" who doesn't need other people (is he saying: "Hell is other people"?). Merton pushes his seductive rhetoric of solitude over the edge. But another chapter of the book, notes on a novel of Julien Green, ends with a beautiful passage that comes close to Nazarena's vision:

> Law is consistent. Grace is "inconsistent."
> The Cross is the sign of contradiction—destroying the seriousness of the Law, of the Empire, of the armies, of blood sacrifice, and of obsession.
>
> But the magicians keep turning the Cross to their own purposes. Yes, it is for them too a sign of

contradiction: the awful blasphemy of the religious magician who makes the Cross contradict mercy! This of course is the ultimate temptation of Christianity! To say that Christ has locked all the doors, has given one answer, settled everything and departed, leaving all life enclosed in the frightful consistency of a system outside of which there is seriousness and damnation, inside of which there is the intolerable flippancy of the saved—while nowhere is there any place left for the mystery of the freedom of divine mercy which alone is truly serious, and worthy of being taken seriously.[5]

It is easy to connect Thomas Merton with the literary current called "American Critical Romanticism": Emerson, Thoreau, Emily Dickinson, and others, since he referred to them often in his books. Could Nazarena also be compared with these "rugged individualists" and lovers of solitude? Perhaps not, although a phrase from one of Dickinson's poems rings true of Nazarena: "Best things dwell out of sight—The pearl, the just, our thought...."[6] The letters of Sister Nazarena, as I found them in the nuns' archives at Sant'Antonio, were mostly penned on odd scraps of paper, as were Emily Dickinson's poems. Both of them wrote on the backs, insides, and flaps of used envelopes, on the reverse of invoices, ledger pages, and on every sort of wrapping material. Only in the last years of her life did Nazarena, on orders from the abbess, consent to use clean, lined notebooks.

Nazarena's writings were sometimes poetic but utterly unpublishable, and yet utterly clear in what she meant to say.

Nazarena was so clear that an Italian Carmelite nun who wrote a book about her missed the whole point. The nun "translated" Nazarena's writings into flawless Italian, entirely losing their spontaneity and the American or French idioms underlying her solecisms. My English translations are, I presume, grammatically and syntactically correct, because that is the kind of English Nazarena would have written, but her incorrect Italian is perfect for conveying her message. No grammar, no glamor.

3. The Anchoress's Last Rule

During the last year and a half of her life, Nazarena filled many pages of her ruled notebook. She told the story of young Julia, her love and study of music, and her vision of the Man of Sorrows who called her to the desert. I have woven into Part 1 many paragraphs of these autobiographical letters.

During the spring of 1989, the fifty-fifth anniversary of her vision, the anchoress wrote another rule (her tenth, or perhaps her twelfth?), no longer a *Regolamento* but now only "notes, points," *appunti*. Sister Nazarena wrote them only for herself; no other nun, she said, was to imitate her way of life.

And yet other monastics (even a cenobite like myself, or a lay person, or a secular priest) can avail themselves of these "notes," because they grew out of inspired Scripture, the only language fit to describe and guide the life of an artist or a saint. They are the substance of her prophecy.

The Call

The "Notes (incomplete) for a rule"⁷ open with a dialogue woven from biblical threads, combining direct citation, paraphrase, and appropriation. She initiates the dialogue with a question. After God's reply and promise, she appropriates as her own response the words of the eternal Son in the letter to the Hebrews.

"Lord, what do you want me to do?" [Mk 10:17, 36].

"Come, follow Me!" [Mk 10:21]. "I am going to lead her into the desert and speak to her heart" [Hos 2:16].

"Here I am, Lord, I have come to do Your will" [Heb 10:7].

The vocation to a strict and perpetual reclusion is God's call to the life of prayer and penitence. The anchoress lives alone with God, in silence, solitude, and hiddenness pushed to their utter limits. In a narrow cell she imitates the solitary life of the desert.

There the anchoress immolates herself without ever seeing or desiring to see any fruit whatever of her immolation. For she lives under the gaze of God alone, for God's glory and the sanctification and salvation of souls, in intimate union with Jesus her redeemer and Mary the co-redeemer. She follows their redemptive journey all the way up Calvary. Mindful of the words "Cut off from me you can do nothing" [Jn 15:5], she makes God's strength the mainstay of her weakness, and says, "There is nothing I cannot do in the One who strengthens me. I know in whom I have put my trust," on whom I have cast my lot, in time and in eternity [Phil 4:13; 2 Tm 1:12].

The Cell

The walls of Nazarena's cell were unpainted, and she wanted no varnished furniture. But the room is not "rustic"; it is simply drab. Above all it is not sound-proofed, and all the noises of the convent and the street can be heard, only slightly softened, through the cracks in the walls and the casement (Nazarena seldom complained about this, and then only to ask that they stucco the cracks). Sant'Antonio is a very cenobitic monastery; while it is a quiet place, the nuns do not follow an absolute rule of silence, and they can engage in noisy banter when at work or in moments of recreation. Both work and recreation are held in the large hall called the lavoriero, *adjoining Nazarena's cell. Mother Ildegarde's room was next to hers.*

"All the days of my life I shall dwell" in the cell of reclusion, always alone with God alone, until I die [Ps 23:6]. "Here shall I rest forevermore, here shall I make my home as I have wished" [Ps 132:14]. "The measuring-line marks out for me a delightful place" [Ps 16:6].

The cell must reflect the poverty of Bethlehem and the nudity of the desert.... There is no table or chair or bed, only a low wooden stool. The anchoress kneels on the bare floor or on a footstool, if the marble is too cold. A board on her knees serves as a table. Instead of a bed, she sleeps on a large box, upon whose cover is nailed a broad cross....

In the vestibule there is a shelf for leaving supplies. In the inside door to the vestibule there is a grating, covered with opaque canvas.

The Spiritual Atmosphere

The subtitle "spiritual atmosphere" is my invention, but it should be clear that Sister Nazarena's paragraphs on "reclusion" and "silence" do not describe particular "ascetical practices" but convey the global sense of her life as an anchoress, which is a relationship with God in faith and an imitation of the silence of Jesus and Mary.

Reclusion: "You must look for the things that are above," not those of the earth, for "the life you have is hidden with Christ in God" [Col 3:2-4].

"I shall have faith and not be afraid, for the Lord is my strength and my song" [Is 12:2].

The anchoress may never go out of her reclusion, nor may anyone enter, unless for some indispensable and urgent necessity—in this case, she covers her eyes with her veil.

Silence: "Jesus was silent" [Mt 26:63]. "As for Mary, she treasured all these things and pondered them in her heart" [Lk

2:19, 51]. "In silence and hope shall be your strength" [Is 30:15; 7:4-9]. "Be quick to listen but slow to speak" [Jas 1:19].

"A heart in silence is a melody for the Heart of God. The sanctuary lamp burns noiselessly before the tabernacle, and incense rises in silence up to the throne of the Savior: Such is the silence of love."[8]

Since exterior silence is worth little or nothing without interior silence, the anchoress must ever be watchful to silence the voices of the world and of creatures, but especially her own voice, so as to give herself totally to a recollected and adoring silence, waiting and listening for the silent and eloquent voice of God.

As a sacrifice she has given up forever all contact with her dear family and all her relatives. She will never be able to see them, hear their voices, or receive any correspondence or news, not even through others.

When she has to speak with someone, she does it through a grate in her door, covered with an opaque piece of cloth. She may speak only with superiors and her spiritual father, with the Sister who brings the items she needs, with the infirmarian, and with workers (in the event repairs have to be made on the cell).

She exchanges letters only with superiors and the spiritual father. For material necessities she may write brief notes to the Sisters.

Prayer

It may surprise some readers, even monastics, that Sister Nazarena said no other vocal prayers than the Divine Office, and that she allotted only one-half hour daily for "spiritual reading" (in today's "mitigated observance," the Camaldolese customary invites the monk to dedicate at least forty-five minutes to lectio divina, with the strong encouragement of longer periods). Note the last paragraph of this section: For "sufficient motive," work can take the place of reading or prayer. However, this deemphasis on the "quantity" of prayer should surprise no one. The anchoritic life in its totality is prayer; its goal is the constant mindfulness of, and conversation with, the Holy Trinity.

"It is good to give thanks to the Lord, to sing praise to your name, O most high, to proclaim your love in the morning, your faithfulness through the watches of the night" [Ps 92:2–3].

"Pray for one another; heartfelt prayer has great power" [Jas 5:16]. "Ask, because whoever asks shall receive" [Mt 7:7–8].

The anchoress prays the Divine Office in union with the heavenly and earthly choirs. The Office, chanted and read, is her only vocal prayer. She rises at 1:00 a.m. for the night vigil.

Silent prayer: Jesus "went up into the hills by Himself to pray" [Mt 14:23; Jn 6:15]. Pleasing to God is the silent, adoring prayer of a loving heart. From one to three in the morning she prays in silence, before and after the Vigil Office. Since "God loves a cheerful giver" [2 Cor 9:7], she tries to make her whole life a silent love song, in union with the eternal song which the Word sings in the Father's bosom, together with the heavenly choirs in everlasting glory.

Reading: "Your word is a lamp for my feet, a light on my path" [Ps 119:105]. Come, O Teacher of teachers, send from heaven a ray of your light, O Brightness most blessed.[9]

Each day she tries to spend at least one-half hour at spiritual reading. She reads slowly and attentively, so that it becomes a deep meditation under the Holy Spirit's guidance, as she listens for God's inspirations and illuminations. She greatly desires to be enlightened, instructed, and guided in seeking and penetrating divine Truth and in nourishing herself with heavenly food.

She may omit spiritual reading and even some prayer, when the work or other tasks give her sufficient motive to do so.

Fasting, Work, and Penitential Practices

Traditional ascetical jargon names "the world, the flesh, and the devil" as the soul's chief enemies. Nazarena habitually replaced the term flesh with ego—there is no trace of "contempt for the body," at least on a theoretical level. Nevertheless, her penitential practices arouse some doubt in our minds. With good reason, most contemporary monastics react with disgust and the suspicion of perverted instincts at the sight of instruments of self-torture. Since the Second Vatican Council, the church's magisterium has redirected our attention from body-punishing practices to new forms of abstaining and renouncing, which truly express and effect conversion of heart. This constant conversion was, of course, the only thing Nazarena was seeking through her ascetical disciplines.

"My food is to do the will of the One who sent me" [Jn 4:34]. "All you who are thirsty, come with joy to the waters" [Is 55:1, 12:3]. "Let anyone who is thirsty come to me; from the heart of the one who believes in me shall flow streams of living water" [Jn 7:37–38]. "Anyone who sows sparsely will reap sparsely as well—and anyone who sows generously will reap generously as well" [2 Cor 9:6].

The anchoress regulates her nourishment under the control of the spiritual father, according to the following norms:

She always drinks water only, except in case of sickness or need. Always prohibited are meat, eggs, fish, butter, and every kind of dessert.

Sundays, feast days, Thursdays, and during the octaves of Christmas and Easter, she takes one or more of the following foods: bread, cooked greens, beans and lentils (or ground lentils), fruit, jam. Cheese is optional, outside Advent and Lent, on Sundays, feast days, and during the octaves of Christmas and Easter.

On the other five weekdays she takes only bread and water, but on Tuesdays and Saturdays, in case of need, she may take one or more of the following: salt, oil, milk (powdered or even fresh), fruit.

In case of illness, she may increase the quantity but not the quality of food. During Advent and Lent, with the help of God and the advice of her spiritual father, she may limit her nourishment more strictly.

Penitential practices: "Remembering the mercies of God, offer your bodies as a living sacrifice, dedicated and acceptable to God" [Rom 12:1]. "You will have to suffer only for a little while: The God of all grace who called you to eternal glory in Christ will restore you, will confirm, strengthen, and support you" [1 Pt 5:10]. "The salvation of many souls depends on the voluntary mortifications practiced by other souls" (Pius XII).

Her penitential practices are under the control of her spiritual father. She does a little more or less according to the liturgical seasons, so as to unite her practice to the spirit of the church, to live more intimately the mysteries of the faith, and to avoid doing them out of habit.

She performs them with joy, gratitude, in a spirit of reparation and love of neighbor..."to make up, in her own body, all the hardships that still have to be undergone by Christ for the sake of his body, the Church" [Col 1:24]. She focuses her attention not on the isolated cross, but rather on the cross seen against the backdrop of the resurrection. She contemplates the glory of the risen Redeemer, who saves souls by the victory of His redemptive sacrifice....

Work: "Work not halfheartedly" [Rom 12:11]. "You go into my vineyard too" [Mt 20:7]. "Whatever you say or do, let it be in the name of the Lord Jesus, in thanksgiving to God the Father through him" [Col 3:17]. "When you have done all you have been told to do, say, 'We are useless servants: We have done no more than our duty'" [Lk 17:10].

She will always be on guard, lest she remain idle a single instant. She will strive to transmute the hours of work into intimate union with God, with Jesus, into hours of contemplation, inner listening, and intercession, according to the attraction and inspiration of the present moment.... She will work with right intention and accuracy, so that what she produces will be well made and completed on schedule.

Clothing: "They put on sackcloth" [Jon 3:5; Lk 11:32]. She wears a robe of sackcloth and a veil of white muslin. She wears no stockings. She sews, washes, and mends her own clothing.

The Virtues of an Anchoress

Nazarena's sense of divine grace was too strong for her ever to fall into the trap of spiritual athleticism. The hard testing of the eleven years before finding the "desert" of her definitive reclusion cured her forever of the vice of presumption, that is, taking virtues for granted. No virtue was for her an "achievement," but all was grace, all was a free gift of God.

Love: "Love binds up all perfectly" [Col 3:14]. "There is no greater love than giving your life for your enemies" [Mt 5:44-45 together with Jn 15:13]. "Even if I spoke the language of the angels, but had no love, I would be only a clanging cymbal" [1 Cor 13:1]. "Even if I gave my body to be burned, and yet had no love, it would avail me naught" [1 Cor 13:3]. "At the evening of life, I shall be judged by love."[10]

Love gets us across the border to eternity. It is the passport to our heavenly country.

The anchoress prays for the grace of total self-forgetfulness, so as to immolate herself totally in the sight of God alone, for the love of God and of souls. Her immolation—which in itself is worthless—gains value and becomes divine through union with the immolation of the immaculate Lamb.

Humility: "God opposes the proud but bestows grace on the humble" [Jas 4:6]. "Because I was of little account, I was pleasing to the Lord" [Dt 7:7-8]. "Never have we looked for honor from human beings" [1 Thes 2:6]. "The Lord has thwarted the plans of the proud, has cast down the mighty from their thrones, and to high places has raised the lowly" [Lk 1:51-52]....

Now and then she will reread these passages, so that they may leave their mark more and more upon her, lest her solitary and penitential life, being infiltrated unawares by vainglory, ambition, pride, and self-complacency, fall prey to a culpable sterility and fail to bear fruit.

O Humility, ground and guardian of the virtues, "keep me as the apple of your eye!" [Ps 17:8].

Obedience: "Whoever listens to you, listens to me" [Lk 10:16].

"For our sake Christ became obedient unto death, even death on a cross" [Phil 2:8].

"Behold, I am the handmaid of the Lord, be it done to me according to your word" [Lk 1:38].

"Jesus went down to Nazareth with his parents and was subject to them" [Lk 2:51].

The Holy Spirit is the Superior of the anchoress's cell; our Lady is her abbess and novice mistress. She will always be mindful and docile in obedience to them.

She will show glad and ready obedience to superiors and her spiritual father, faithfully observing her rule out of love, doing everything in the sight of God, for God and souls, in intimate union with Jesus her Redeemer and Mary the coredemptress, to share in their great work of salvation.

She will always pay close attention to the little things. It is easy to neglect them, and gradually one falls away, without realizing it, into laxity and negligence. "Anyone who is trustworthy in little things is trustworthy in great" [Lk 16:10].

Keeping Watch

One of the principal characteristics of universal monasticism—Hindu, Buddhist, Essene, as well as Christian—is the discipline of time. Nazarena's ordered schedule frames this characteristic in the Gospel understanding of "realized eschatology," with its sense of serene urgency.

"Stay awake, because you do not know either the day or the hour" [Mt 25:13]. "Blessed that servant whom the master, arriving in the night, will find keeping watch" [Mt 24:46].

The anchoress submits her daily schedule to her spiritual father for his approval and blessing. She follows it faithfully, without considering whether she feels like doing what it prescribes or not. Since the schedule has been approved by one who represents God, she deems it an expression of God's will moment by moment, and so it is a powerful brake on her self-will. Living as she does in solitude, the schedule is a divine mainstay against the tyranny and the exhausting volubility of caprice, passion, etcetera.

On awakening, she resumes her ascent of the mountain of pure love, under the loving gaze of Jesus [Mk 10:21], the supernatural Sun that illumines, purifies, strengthens, admonishes, instructs, and makes peaceful, happy, and holy her life alone with him. Limited is the time of this mortal life; therefore she strives not to waste a single instant thinking about the past, which can never return, nor about the future, which she cannot know. She focuses her attention on the decisive moment of time present, ignoring appearances, pleasant or unpleasant, and with a loving and trusting surrender accepts either alternative as the gift which God the heavenly Father judges best for her. "All things work together for the good of those who love God" [Rom 8:28].

Especially in times of darkness and pain, she keeps ever in mind that each hour spent digging deep in the mine of this earthly exile yields incalculable, eternal riches for the help and salvation of souls, provided she generously exploits each moment, instead of gracelessly wasting it.

In the Shadow of Death

In previous versions of her Regolamento, Nazarena *gave precise dispositions for her death (she wanted to die alone, like Saint Romuald) and for her burial. Now she no longer seeks to have power even over her own body. Perhaps she foresees that she will pass from this life in the next few months (on the memorial of Saint Romuald, February 7, 1990), and that she will want her Sisters to be with her.*

"Have mercy on me, O God, in your kindness; in your goodness blot out my sins" [Ps 51:3]. "My trust is in you, Lord; I say, you are my God, every moment of my life is in your hands" [Ps 31:14-15]. "A broken, a contrite heart, O God, you never scorn" [Ps 51:17]. "To your hands I commit my spirit" [Ps 31:5]. "I shall sing the faithful love of the Lord forever" [Ps 89:1].

As in life, so in death: to make little, persevering efforts, relying on grace, to live and die loving, unknown and hidden, alone with God, and then to take flight on wings of love to the kingdom of Love.

"Was it not necessary that the Christ should suffer before entering into his glory?" [Lk 24:26].

"He has given you an example, that you might do as he did" [1 Pt 2:2; Jn 13:15].

"Nothing is impossible in the eyes of God" [Gn 18:14; Jer 32:27; Lk 1:37].

"Behold, I am coming" [Ps 40:8; Heb 10:7].

"Jesus...loved them to the end" [Jn 13:1].

"It is fulfilled" [Jn 19:30].

"Even if you have to die, keep faithful" [Rv 2:10].

Yes, almighty God, through Jesus and Mary with the Holy Spirit.

Amen. Alleluia.

APPENDIX
The Story of Sant'Antonio

In the nuns' archives, while studying the letters of Sister Nazarena, I came across a manuscript dated 1764. The anonymous author, a Camaldolese monk, recounted the life of the nuns' foundress, Mother Angela of Saint Peter, née Angela Francesca Pezza, from her birth to her burial at San Gregorio in 1758. Reading it, I became convinced it should be included in this book, because the story of Nazarena's Sisters gives an insight into why they accepted an American anchoress into their midst.

On the seventeenth of May, 1687, a wealthy couple of silk-weavers, Giácomo Pezza and Órsola Ferrari, stood at the baptismal font of Saint Peter's in the Vatican, as their second daughter, three days old, received the sacramental graces and the names Angela Francesca. The child would hardly remember her father and the comfortable life his fine silk fabrics provided the family, for he died shortly after her fourth birthday. A year later Órsola married a man by the name of Ferdinando, and no more than four years had gone by when she was again a widow, this time without the means to maintain her three daughters. She placed Angela in a boarding school for orphan girls, attached to the pope's Lateran palace.

"God endowed Angela," wrote the anonymous monk, "with special graces, which showed themselves in her sweet, modest, and obedient character. Her companions called her 'Angela the Judicious' and looked up to her as their teacher, although she was only thirteen years old. The other girls willingly took part in the religious services she organized, when she would read to them from some devout book, and then, standing on a chair, would preach a sermon."

Angela was eighteen when she was orphaned of her mother. The chaplain of the boarding school, perhaps jealous of Angela's sermons, forbade her to enter a convent. A marriage was arranged, and in 1705 Angela became the wife of a land surveyor from Ancona, Francesco Bruzzesi. A devout man himself, he allowed his wife to turn their home into a monastery, where she continued to read devout books and observe fasts. She did not love being a man's wife, but she treated him with respect and even a certain affection. She apologized to him: "Forgive me, Francesco, for not doing things the way you want and for not being your servant, as a dutiful wife is supposed to be. I was not made for worldly life, but God willed that I marry—may he be blessed forever!"

They had three children, Sebastiano, Gian Paolo, and a daughter she named Órsola, after her mother. The children became Angela's novices, although none of them would remain with her in monastic life. Even Francesco took part in the recitation of the Little Office of the Virgin, and he listened willingly to Angela's readings and meditations. But his life too was brief; he was only thirty-three when he died, and his widow was twenty-nine.

While still in mourning, Angela was surrounded with suitors, interested in her beauty and her late husband's wealth. She rejected their proposals and remained at home, concerned only with raising her children and finding her way into religious life. Her confessor at the time was a Franciscan; she also frequented the Passionist friars at the church of Saints John and Paul on the Coelian Hill. One day Angela was on her way there to attend mass, when she thought of visiting a sick friend. The woman detained her, and when she arrived at the church, she found the doors closed. So she walked down the hill to San Gregorio, where the lay brother at the entrance to the monastery told her that a late mass would be celebrated that morning. She asked if she could speak to a priest, and the brother went to call don Alfonso Eufemi, who heard her confession and then offered mass.

Angela felt at ease with the gentle monk, and after the service she thanked the Lord for leading her there. But uncertain whether to take him as her regular confessor, she let four weeks pass before returning to San Gregorio.

Don Alfonso was impressed with his new penitent. All the monks admired the devout young widow, almost daily at mass, who would kneel for hours before the ancient icon of the Virgin in the side chapel, her eyes wet with tears. At home she kept a rigorous, monastic regime of fasts, all-night vigils, and prayers, with regular visits to the sick and the poor, whom she cared for with her own hands. Soon her two sons were old enough to leave home, and don Alfonso helped her find them suitable employment, so that she might be free to take vows as a Camaldolese Benedictine oblate. He counseled her to proceed without haste and obliged her to seek the advice of two eminent theologians. Neither of them was as impressed with Angela as was her confessor, and they severely questioned her idea of founding a community of monastic oblates. But in the end her gentle and prudent answers overcame their diffidence.

Don Alfonso was convinced of her vocation, as was the abbot of San Gregorio. On the feast of the Immaculate Conception, December 8, 1722, they clothed Angela in the habit of a Camaldolese nun, authorizing her to remain at her home in the Campo Boario during the novitiate year. A few months later don Alfonso and the abbot accompanied five young women to her home and placed them under her direction.

At the end of the year Mother Angela and her postulants

established a women's oblate retreat. The project met with immediate opposition on the part of ecclesiastical authorities and encountered a number of practical obstacles as well. Six years as a widow had depleted Mother Angela's inheritance. She was unable to support the nascent community on her small income, and the house in the Campo Boario facing the slaughterhouse was unsuitable for a monastery. With trust in God and immense patience she overcame Vatican opposition, and on the first of March, 1724, she and her five postulants moved to a quiet side street overlooking the ruins of the Roman Forum, ten minutes' walk from San Gregorio. On the second Sunday of Easter, Mother Angela professed solemn monastic vows in the hands of the abbot, and the following December her five companions were clothed in white monastic robes at the high altar of San Gregorio, while the monks chanted the Psalms of Vespers.

The first of the novices was Angela's own daughter, Órsola; her request to join the new community was motivated more by natural affection than by divine vocation. Mother Angela eventually gave her daughter a dowry and arranged a marriage, while the other four candidates of more mature age remained. The life at the retreat was anything but easy; none of the women had personal wealth, and although they spent long hours working at various crafts, had their neighbors not supplied them with food, they would not have been able to see out the year of their novitiate.

Theirs was a genuine monastic life, although not subject to the strict laws of enclosure. Each day, after chanting the pre-dawn Hours of Matins and Lauds, they left the retreat and walked the short distance through the ancient Forum to sing mass with the monks at San Gregorio. On the eve of Christmas, 1726, Mother Angela's four companions professed their vows in the presence of don Alfonso. His Christmas gift to them was a document of the Holy See granting them a consecrated altar in their small chapel, where mass might be offered daily.

The community began to grow. They opened a boarding school for girls, several of whom chose to join the community. Once more they were obliged to move, this time to a modest house at the foot of the Janiculum, near Saint Peter's. The Holy See confirmed their status as nuns, although the restrictions of cloister were not applied to them in full. They continued to frequent San Gregorio, and when Mother Angela died in 1758, at the age of seventy-one, she was buried in a side chapel of the monks' church. A few years later, the community inherited a convent near the basilica of Saint Mary Major on the Esquiline hill, and the foundress's remains were transfered there, in the chapel where today the Russian-rite Jesuits chant their Slavonic liturgies.

On the Esquiline

In the year following the birth of the United States, the Camaldolese monastic oblates became the nuns of Saint Antony of Egypt, from the title of the knightly order to which the convent had previously belonged. When they moved there, the eldest among them remembered Mother Angela's prophecies. She had told them that neither where they were then living, nor in a building yet to be constructed, would they find their home, but in a monastery already existing in the city. At the Convent of the Hospitallers of Saint Antony—into which she as a woman could never have entered—they found her description of the house exact to the smallest details.

These were times of war and great upheaval in Rome and throughout Europe. In 1777 the eternal city and much of the central Italian peninsula were directly subject to papal governance; after France, the States of the Church would be one of the first countries to recognize the independence of the thirteen American colonies. The new nation promptly exchanged ambassadors with the Holy See. Then France, which had gained nothing from her recognition of the United States, was torn apart by revolution, which led to the epoch of Napoleon and his conquests.

Few orders in the Catholic Church were as hard hit by the Napoleonic suppression of monasteries as were the Camaldolese monks and nuns. Camaldoli itself barely survived, thanks to its physical isolation in the Tuscan Apennines; four priests were allowed to remain there during the dozen years of suppression. Although they were forbidden to wear their white monastic robes, they continued to sing the Psalms of the Benedictine Office, and a lone lay brother at the Eremo rang the great bell day and night to announce the liturgical Hours.

The nuns of Sant'Antonio were not so fortunate. Their recently acquired monastery was in a busy quarter on the Esquiline hill. They lived quietly within its walls, welcoming the simple faithful on Saint Antony's feast, January 17, for the traditional blessing of horses and other livestock. An admirer wrote, "Although the nuns uttered few words, the affability of their heart was revealed in their smiling faces. They lived in the peace of God, they loved their work, and they died serenely as they lived, with the words of the Psalm [122:1] on their lips, 'What joy when they told me the news: We are going up to the Lord's house.'"

The rage of Napoleon and his men descended on these quiet nuns in the summer of 1809. The abbess called the nuns together, spoke words of encouragement, and gave each a small sum of money from the community's modest savings. They were twenty; thirteen of them, native to different parts of Italy, received from the Napoleonic governor the promise of a miserable pension and were told to return to their homes. Three had family in Rome and could stay with them; the abbess and three nuns who had no home to go to were given lodging in the city by the Countess Caterina Mazzagalli.

They remained guests of the countess for more than five years. Her palace had its chapel, where nonjuror priests came secretly to say mass. "They abode in constant prayer, anxiously awaiting God's mercy," wrote the chronicler of Sant'Antonio, voicing the nuns' hope that the lesson of Napoleon's rise and fall might not be lost on later generations. After the restitution of the papal states, when the abbess summoned her Sisters to return to the monastery, only three responded; the others could not, having already met their heavenly Spouse in death.

The Countess Mazzagalli would not let her guests languish in discouragement. High connections with the papal administration enabled her to ransom the nuns' property, successfully contesting the pretensions of a man who had purchased the building from Napoleon's governor. On November 15, 1814, the abbess received the keys to the monastery, but she found most of the upper floor without a roof, the windows bare of glass, and the ground floor covered with piles of debris. A sum of money from the papal deputy enabled them to clear the rubble and render habitable one wing of the monastery. The seven surviving nuns could once more don their habits and sing a solemn *Te Deum* in the restored choir. But the church was still in shambles, and the winter winds penetrated every angle of the house. Finally the countess's pleas reached the ears of the papal treasurer, who provided a sum sufficient for a complete reconstruction of the monastery.

At last the nuns could taste the quiet joy of their regular liturgies, but their joy was soon chilled by news that all government welfare would be withdrawn from religious congregations, which henceforth would have to establish their own endowment by selling properties acquired over the decades and centuries past. The nuns of Sant'Antonio had neither lands nor endowment; they wept at what seemed the ultimate dissolution of their community, due not to Napoleonic violence but to the harsh policies of a bankrupt papal state.

Once more the good countess was the Sisters' savior, and she returned to the Vatican to plead with the treasurer. He raised one objection after another, until at last he was won over to their cause. Four nuns of another Benedictine community, which could not be reopened after the suppression, would join those of Sant'Antonio, bringing with them the endowment of their former monastery.

These eleven aging nuns, whom a miraculous providence had preserved from closure by secular and ecclesiastical powers, received twenty novices in the course of less than ten years. What drew the candidates was not a comfortable life, for the physical accommodations of the nuns were anything but comfortable. They were attracted by the luminous virtues of a Sister who was neither abbess nor novice mistress, but rather in charge of the infirmary and the pantry. The kind and attentive manner of Sister Gertrude of the Blessed Sacrament won the hearts of all, from the superior to the youngest novice, and when the abbess who had led the community through the wasteland passed away, the nuns unanimously chose Sister Gertrude as her successor.

The year was 1828, and a Camaldolese monk, Placido Zurla, was in the Vatican as cardinal vicar for the diocese of Rome. In less than three years another Camaldolese, Mauro Cappellari, became Pope Gregory XVI, the last pope to our day who belonged to a religious order.

Not even a century and a half have been time enough for historians to disentangle the paradox of this enervated monastic congregation thrust by conflicting powers to the summit of the Catholic hierarchy. Gregory, so "conservative" that his successor, Pius IX, was initially viewed as a "liberal," was the first pope in the history of Christendom to condemn slavery as a crime against humanity. Ancestor of today's environmentalists, he forbade the construction of the railroad in his papal states. Apologist of infallibility, he erected the mission in South India where a century later Jules Monchanin, Henri Le Saux, and Bede Griffiths would dream of incorporating the best of Hinduism into the Catholic Church. A member of the most provincial of Benedictine families, Pope Cappellari founded California's first

diocese of Monterey, where today the Camaldolese Benedictines of Big Sur join in the "Four Winds Council" with
Native Americans, Zen Buddhists, and the latter-day Are-
opagites of Esalen Institute, to converse about new paradigms
in science, theology, and mysticism. A papacy of sheer paradox, Gregory's reign can be understood only within the logic
that links Saint Benedict's stability and discretion to Saint
Romuald's itinerant hermit life—if indeed we may deem logi-
cal the eschatological extremism of contemplative saints.

The pontificate of don Mauro Cappellari did more harm
than good to the Camaldolese Benedictines. Cardinal Zurla's
only favor to his nuns at Sant'Antonio was to grant them strict
papal enclosure. The hardware required by papal law to hide
these affable sisters from profane view—bars on windows and
doors, wrought-iron grillwork in parlor and chapel—was to be
provided at the nuns' own expense, although Cardinal Zurla
did promise them matching funds.

Gregory XVI's meek but adamant refusal to take sides
among Europe's powers paved the way for the providential
end of the Holy See's territorial dominion. His successor, Pius
IX, would see Cavour and Garibaldi lead Italy to statehood
and the House of Savoy to the Quirinal Palace, from which the
papal monarchy once ruled the eternal city and its outlying
domains. Gregory's own Camaldolese, along with all the
other monastics who had successfully regrouped after
Napoleon, would again suffer suppression and dispossession
under the Italian state.

The brief period of the "Roman Republic," 1848–1849, gave
the nuns a foretaste of evils to come, with orders to open their
gates and allow inventories of their furnishings and goods.
When in September 1870 Rome became Italy's capitol and Pope
Pius IX "the prisoner of the Vatican," the new civil authorities
proceeded with the expropriation of ecclesiastical properties.
The pope's response was an intransigent refusal to cooperate; he
gave orders that, in virtue of their vow of obedience, religious

were to open their cloisters only to physical force. There was no question of compromise with the new regime.

The nuns of Sant'Antonio obeyed these orders, of course, and the abbess, named Angela like the foundress, was inflexible. She had known Pius IX personally when he was a young priest; as pope he visited the monastery several times. However, the motivations of the nuns were anything but ideological; they were not, like other intransigents, dreamers of the Middle Ages or of the *ancien régime*. For them it was simply a monastic question that concerned their sense of belonging to the Body of Christ and their vow of obedience.

1871: The Suppression of Sant'Antonio

The following chronicle, by an anonymous nun of Sant'Antonio, gives a ground-level view of the Italian suppression and the papacy's response to it. This is micro-history; it places before our eyes the violence done to these women by all the contenders, the pope no less than his adversaries. You can still take sides if you wish, but in any case, you are bound to conclude that the intransigence of opposing parties produced tragic effects in the lives of the real protagonists of the story: the general population, both lay and religious.

After the usurpation of Rome, all the religious communities were seized with trepidation, knowing what unfavorable principles and laws inspired the new government. The nuns of Sant'Antonio enjoyed only a few more months of tranquillity. On July 26, 1871, they were visited by an entrepreneur who said he wanted to purchase their garden. Arguing that it was impossible for them to sell it, the abbess sent him to the papal deputy for cloistered religious.

Two days later a letter arrived from city hall informing the nuns that on the thirty-first of the month an engineer with three assistants would come to survey and assess the garden.

On that date, at 7:00 A.M., with the written permission of the cardinal vicar, they came to inspect the premises. They told the nuns they would return the following day, as they did— five men with all the equipment necessary for the survey, which they completed in two hours.

For a few more days the government left the nuns alone to worry about their future. Then on August 18 the abbess heard that a semi-official newspaper had just announced the royal decree for the expropriation of the Monastery of Saint Antony; a letter from the government soon confirmed the news.

On August 31 two members of the royal commission for expropriations came to inspect the property, but since they bore no written authorization, they were sent away. The following day they came with written instructions from the cardinal to the mother abbess, and she, stating that she was yielding only to a show of force, allowed them to enter the cloister. They went through the whole house and made a list of the rooms. On September 5 a royal decree was placed in the hands of the abbess by a court functionary, and two days later other men came to complete the inspection of the house, saying they would return on the morrow. Forewarned, the abbess made it known that no one would be allowed to enter without written authorization from Colonel Garavaglia, the officer in charge of expropriations. When three men arrived—a notary public, an architect, and a surveyor—she politely but firmly sent them off. They left with the threat to make a report to the commission, and no more than an hour passed before they were back with a letter from the colonel. The nuns were again obliged to yield to force, but the men were admitted only on the arrival of the father confessor and a trusted friend of the monastery.

The week following September 11 saw the architect and his surveyor in the cloister every day, "to assess," they said, "the entire property in accordance with orders from the government." On the twelfth, Colonel Garavaglia himself came, and after sticking his nose into every corner of the monastery, including the attic, he declared that he had orders to establish a military hospital there, with three hundred beds. And since one visit was not enough to inspect everything, he said he would be sending someone to draw up floor plans, so that he could study the layout and then inform them of his decision. "In the meantime," he said, "you should remain tranquil."

A few days later he sent a couple of men bearing his letter. At this point the cardinal wrote, ordering the nuns, in the Holy Father's name, to dismiss the gentlemen drawing up the plans and to forbid entrance to all government officials. The abbess fulfilled her obligation to inform the two men of the pope's orders, to which they replied with the citation of the royal decree.

"Such orders are valid for you, not for me," declared the abbess.

The engineer asked her, "Must we then enter only by force of arms?"

"Yes, only thus!" she answered.

The man in charge of the survey, seeing how resolute she was, could do no more than send word to the royal commission and leave. At 7:30 A.M. the following day a letter came from Colonel Garavaglia demanding a written explanation of the abbess's behavior. She immediately replied as follows:

"I inform you, sir, that my refusal to admit the persons charged with surveying the monastery was no arbitrary act on my part, but was in response to an absolute order from the Holy Father himself. Hence I was obliged to answer in those very terms."

At 9:00 that same morning an architect, his young assistant, and a notary public appeared on their doorstep, ostensibly to hear from the abbess's own mouth the terms of the orders she had received. They listened and feigned submission, saying that the mother superior was certainly in the right, and that they could not but praise her behavior. "However," they continued, "we are sorry to inform you that the government intends the survey to be completed peacefully, just as it was begun. Your refusal to allow us to do so will only cause disturbance for the community."

To which the abbess replied, "I and my Sisters are quite ready to endure whatever unpleasant consequences may come upon us, provided we do not fail of our vows, in first place that of obedience to the Head of the Church."

For several days the nuns remained in quiet trepidation, unsure of their end. On the last day of September, Colonel Garavaglia asked the abbess to delegate a person of her choice with whom he might arrange for the removal of their persons and their belongings from the monastery, whose expropriation was to be concluded forthwith.

A few days later, a papal knight, Mr. Pietro Azzurri, with orders from his eminence the cardinal vicar, sought an appointment with the colonel and energetically informed him that it was impossible to comply with his instructions, given the pope's absolute prohibition to yield to anything but physical force.

The colonel was unmoved by Azzurri's statement. His only message for the nuns was that they must leave the monastery. "Tell them to pack up and get out," he said, again and again.

Azzurri went to the Vatican and informed the Holy Father of his conversation with Colonel Garavaglia, to which the pope repeated his order to the nuns that they not yield but to force, and striking the floor with his cane, said three times, "Let the colonel's men break down the door with hatchets!"

On October 2, a delegation from the expropriations ministry went to the cardinal vicar to see if they could wrest from him some expression of consent. He would not even acknowledge their request. He politely scolded them, but by now all words were useless. Four days later, at forty-five minutes past midnight, the nuns received word from Colonel Garavaglia that at 7:30 that same morning he and his men would take possession of the monastery, in accordance with the law.

Imagine, if you can, the poor nuns' anguish and terror at the final news, and how they must have spent the last hours of that night. The moment they received the colonel's midnight message they sent word to his eminence, and they asked Mr. Azzurri and another gentleman, Vincenzo Guidi, to come defend the nuns when the colonel's men arrived to attack the monastery. By 5:00 there were wagons full of tools and ladders in front of their door, and at 7:00 Azzurri and Guidi were there to await the fateful moment. They had not long to wait, because at 7:30 sharp a company of thirty men, with Colonel Garavaglia at their head, stood at the entrance to the monastery: Officers of the corps of engineers, notaries public, architects, and various anonymous rascals were demanding to speak with the nuns' representatives.

The two papal knights came forward, and the crowd yelled, "Open the door!"

They responded calmly, "You already know the Holy Father's orders; we cannot comply with your request."

At that the colonel said, "Call the abbess!"

She was standing just inside the door; immediately she came forward, accompanied by two of the senior nuns. It was a miracle of God that they did not faint but remained standing, intrepid in the face of those thirty men.

The colonel ordered the abbess to open the door. She firmly replied, "We shall yield only to force."

He repeated, "Open the door, or we'll break it down. You have twenty-four hours to pack up and get out."

The poor abbess pleaded with him. "Give us at least two weeks!" she said.

All was in vain. The colonel assumed command of the men and ordered them, "Break in through the garden gate." The abbess went and barred the way. At that the police commissioner put on his sash and said three times, "In the name of the law, mother abbess, I command you to open the door." And each time she answered that the laws of cloister and the express orders of the Holy Father forbade her to comply in any way with his request, that she was yielding only to force, and that she was not responsible for their violation of the cloister.

The colonel terminated the discussion: "Break down the door," he said. Azzurri and Guidi hurried around to the service entrance so that they could witness the act from within the enclosure. First the government officials came forward, and finding the nuns had locked the door, had their men apply ramrods and crowbars to it. At this point, seeing that all ecclesiastical orders had been fulfilled, Mr. Azzurri himself took the keys from the abbess and opened the door. Garavaglia's men declared themselves in possession of the monastery.

Several times the nuns implored them at least to keep out the crowd that had been drawn to the scene, and finally they shut the door. Having consummated his crime, the colonel turned to the abbess and told her, "Henceforth you shall allow anyone to enter who presents himself in my name." He ordered his men to open the gates and let the wagons in with their tools and other building materials, and the rabble would have overrun the garden, had the nuns' workers not pushed them back.

When the tragedy was concluded and the crowds dispersed, the colonel's men told them to let the architects and engineers in when they came the following Monday to draw up the plans. All government officials were to have free access to the monastery.

The notary public finished writing out his report, and the men made to leave. But the abbess again addressed the colonel, "Please grant us at least eight or ten days to move our belongings." He refused to give her a clear answer, but said, "I'll present your request to the royal commission and let you know what they decide."

Upon their departure the scene changed. The monastery's parlors were filled with well-wishers, clergy, religious, and lay persons, who came to see what had been done to these poor brides of Christ. Everyone expressed concern and offered help. Two days later Colonel Garavaglia wrote: "The royal commission authorizes me to grant you a delay in effecting your evacuation of the monastery. You have exactly eight days, the deadline being Monday, October 16, 1871, at seven o'clock in the morning."

The Nuns Find a New Home

The nuns' exodus first led them to a convent attached to the church of Santa Susanna, now the American church in Rome. The Camaldolese Benedictines shared the premises with another group of refugees, the Cistercians. On February 2, 1873, they were rudely awakened by a letter announcing the expropriation of Santa Susanna. Colonel Garavaglia was again at their door.

The Holy See approached the colonel with the suggestion that, since he had stripped the nuns of everything they possessed, he should at least provide them with a roof over their heads. On this point the law was on the nuns' side. However, the colonel replied that accommodations being scarce in Rome, each of the sisters ought to return to her family. The cardinal searched for a convent where they could remain as a community, but he found no place where all forty-six of them could live together.

At this point the pope himself, out of regard for the monastic sisters of his predecessor Gregory XVI, offered to house them at his summer residence, Castel Gandolfo. The nuns were grateful for the offer, even though it would mean moving outside the city, far from the friendships and the innocent attachments that had sustained them in these difficult times. Aware of this difficulty, the pope suggested another option: They could have an outbuilding on the premises of a retreat house staffed by the Dames of the Sacred Heart, on land belonging to a Roman nobleman at the foot of the Janiculum. The cardinal vicar himself came to invite them there. The abbess accompanied him to see the property, but they both realized that the house simply could not accommodate forty-six nuns.

For a month and a half Colonel Garavaglia left them in peace, but toward the end of March the siege began again in earnest. The nuns had no choice but to ask the Dames of the Sacred Heart to let them add a wing to the house offered for their use, to provide for a kitchen and refectory, above which an attic could serve as a dormitory. In April a slapdash construction was thrown up, and the following month the nuns moved in. Their pain was in part alleviated by the great kindness shown them by the Sacred Heart nuns. The two communities remained separate, but the Camaldolese received much assistance from their hosts, whose circumstances, living as they did on private land under the protection of an aristocratic family, were much more secure.

The nuns were packed into spaces rendered even smaller by the storage of the furnishings and other possessions they had succeeded in moving from the spacious convent on the Esquiline. "Rare were the moments a nun could enjoy a bit of solitude!" exclaimed the chronicler of Sant'Antonio, who went on to tell of the holes in the roof and the cracks in the walls of their precarious lean-to, which rendered urgent another move. The relative peace and quiet of the patrician villa at the foot of the Janiculum was not to be theirs permanently.

The nuns' friend and spokesman Pietro Azzurri came to know of a villa with a large garden on the Aventine, and he initiated talks between the owner and the nuns. But no sooner had the abbess seen the property, than the offer was withdrawn. They were distraught, but they also realized that they had no means to meet the owner's request for the enormous sum of forty thousand *scudi*. When all other directions pointed to dead ends, again Pope Pius IX came to their rescue; he told the cardinal vicar, "I do not wish them to remain in such straits; let them take another look at the house on the Aventine, and if they like it, they are to conclude the purchase immediately."

On January 3, 1878, the abbess and nine senior nuns went to see the property, and although it would require some work to adapt it to monastic use, she told her companions, "This will be our home." The community were overjoyed at the news and began packing their belongings, while Pietro Azzurri had the contract drawn up and signed his name to it, as the nuns' legal representative. The pope gave assurance that the Holy See itself would contribute to the purchase, provided two Vatican prelates added their seals to the contract. But on the feast of Saint Romuald, February 7, the nuns' hopes were again dashed, with the news that the Holy Father had passed away.

"The Lord, who never abandons his own in time of need, came to our aid," wrote the chronicler, "for he inspired his eminence the cardinal vicar to take the matter into his own hands. He had the purchase concluded in his own home, put his name to the contract, and gave the owner the sum of thirty-eight thousand *scudi*." The day was February 23, 1878, and the entire community of Sant'Antonio moved into their new home on the Aventine. These forty-six women had remained together during the hard years of homelessness, and two or three of the youngest would live through two world wars to see Julia Crotta enter Sant'Antonio and make vows as Sister Nazarena. In Julia's eleven years of searching for a desert place, they saw a parable of their own exodus, and they welcomed her gladly.

Notes

PROLOGUE

1. The written documentation on which this book is based consists of hundreds of letters and notes, some very long, others only a few lines regarding work and other practical matters. It would have been impossible to cite them, without a critical edition, a chronology, and an index. So before I began writing, I had to prepare another book, a volume of nearly four hundred pages, containing a representative selection of Nazarena's writings (about a fourth of them) and a few other documents, which I have been able to date with some degree of certitude. The volume, which has yet to be published, is entitled *Gli scritti di Suor Nazarena Julia Crotta, Monaca reclusa camaldolese*. When it is printed, scholars and others interested in the original texts will be able to compare them with the quotations in this book. Each document has been numbered, and the notes will cite my critical edition as "SN," followed by the ordinal number and the page number, for example: SN58, p. 214.

PART ONE

1. SN16, pp. 76-77.
2. 1898 was the same year my grandfather Józef Matusiewicz, fleeing the Russian czar, landed in Philadelphia.

195

3. SN17, p. 78.

4. Ibid., p. 79.

5. SN11, p. 48; cf. SN8, p. 40.

6. SN15, p. 76.

7. SN1, p. 7; SN11, p. 49.

8. SN11, pp. 48-49. Once her mother ordered her sternly to apologize to a person who had taken offense at something Julia had said or done. Convinced that she was in the right, she refused. Maria knew that the most severe punishment for her daughter was being sent to bed without supper, and at Julia's refusal she threatened to do so. Julia said nothing and went to her room. After supper, Maria looked in on her daughter and again asked her to apologize. Julia refused. Bedtime came, and there was Mamma once more, saying, "If you do as I say, I'll bring you supper in bed." Julia's answer was silence. Mamma went out, but after a short time she was back, begging Julia to make her apologies and eat her supper. Silence. Shortly before midnight, Mamma returned, this time carrying a tray with Julia's supper. "Eat," she said, but her daughter was silent. "Eat!" Silence. "EAT!" Julia was motionless. Mamma Maria lifted her hands and eyes to heaven and began to weep softly. Seeing her mothers' tears, Julia grabbed the tray and started wolfing down her supper. Mamma wiped her tears and sighed. Never again would she threaten Julia with being sent to bed without supper.

9. Ibid., p. 52.

10. SN17, p. 79.

11. SN6, p. 36.

12. SN5, p. 24.

13. SN11, pp. 52-53.

14. SN18, p. 81.

15. SN11, p. 52.

16. Ibid., p. 51.

17. SN17, p. 79.

18. SN11, pp. 50-51.

19. SN18, p. 81.
20. SN11, p. 51. Once her classmates threw a party; Julia arrived a little late. The other girls and boys seemed a bit embarrassed the moment she walked in, but then they asked her to play the piano, and the party was a success. Afterward one of the boys offered to walk her home. He told Julia, "You know why everyone stopped talking when you arrived? They were telling jokes that weren't very nice and they knew you didn't want to hear that sort of thing." Julia said nothing, but turned and walked away. In one of her last letters, Nazarena told the abbess this story, and added, "He was a handsome young man with a good character. Strange! I never asked myself why he spoke to me after the party, but now I think he was the one who told the others to stop telling those jokes and to talk about nice things."
21. SN17, p. 80.
22. SN11, p. 53.
23. Ibid.
24. The recital, including works by a number of other women composers, was held at Sprague Hall Auditorium on May 19, 1932, at 3:00 P.M.; the program is in the archives of the Music School Library.
25. SN18, p. 81.
26. SN11, p. 54.
27. SN5, p. 21; SN6, p. 26.
28. SN6, p. 26.
29. The "new creation" theme bridges the two Testaments; see, for example, Is 65:16, 66:22; 2 Pt 3:13; Rv 21:1.
30. SN2, pp. 11–12.
31. SN6, p. 34.
32. SN11, p. 58.
33. Ibid., pp. 54–55.
34. SN18, p. 81.
35. SN11, pp. 55–56.
36. SN8, pp. 40–41.

37. SN11, p. 56.
38. SN14, p. 73.
39. SN5, p. 23.
40. SN6, p. 27.
41. SN11, p. 56.
42. Ibid., p. 57.
43. Ibid.
44. Ibid.
45. SN6, pp. 27-28.
46. SN14, pp. 72-73.
47. SN6, p. 28.
48. Ibid., p. 29.
49. SN11, p. 59.
50. SN4, p. 19.
51. SN11, p. 58.
52. Ibid., p. 59.
53. Ibid.
54. SN6, p. 28.
55. SN11, p. 59.
56. Ibid., p. 60; SN6, p. 29.
57. SN6. p. 29.
58. SN14, p. 73.
59. Ibid., p. 74.
60. SN11, p. 60.
61. Ibid., p. 60; SN5, p. 21; SN6, p. 29.
62. SN6, p. 29; cf. Jn 16:20.
63. SN5, p. 22.
64. SN11, p. 61.
65. SN14, p. 74.
66. SN11, p. 62.
67. SN19, pp. 83-84.
68. SN6, p. 30.
69. SN14, p. 75.
70. SN11, p. 62.
71. Ibid., pp. 62-63.

72. SN9, p. 42.

73. SN14, p. 75. She initially spelled her name "Nazzarena" but later used the Latin spelling "Nazarena"; however, she seldom signed her letters.

74. SN10, pp. 45–46.

75. SN20, p. 86.

76. Ibid., p. 87.

77. From an oral account by don Anselmo.

78. SN46, p. 198.

79. SN47, pp. 200–201.

80. SN24, p. 99.

81. Ibid., p. 100.

82. Ibid., pp. 100–101.

83. SN6, p. 34.

84. SN12, p. 67.

85. SN13, p. 70.

86. SN12, p. 66.

87. Cf. SN48, p. 200.

88. SN20, p. 85.

89. Ibid., p. 86.

90. SN21, p. 88.

91. Ibid., p. 89.

92. Ibid., p. 90.

93. Ibid., pp. 91–92.

94. SN55, pp. 205–207.

95. SN51, pp. 204–205.

96. SN55, p. 210.

97. SN57, pp. 211–214.

98. Ibid., p. 212.

99. SN58, p. 214.

100. See a letter by Mother Ildegarde, SN98, pp. 262–263.

101. Rule of Saint Benedict 68,15.

102. Cf. Rule of Saint Benedict, prologue 49. SN68, pp. 226–227.

103. SN69, p. 228.

104. SN71, pp. 231–232.
105. SN70, p. 229.
106. Ibid.
107. Ibid., p. 230.
108. SN94, pp. 256–257.
109. SN85, pp. 242–243.
110. SN86, pp. 243–244.
111. SN87 pp. 244–245.
112. SN88 p. 245.
113. SN 90, pp. 250–251.
114. SN91, pp. 252–253.
115. SN92, pp. 254–255.
116. SN99, pp. 263–264.
117. Ibid., p. 264.
118. Ibid.
119. SN100, p. 266.
120. SN102, p. 269.
121. SN103, pp. 269–272.
122. SN123, pp. 301–302.
123. Ibid., p. 302.
124. SN124, pp. 303–304.
125. SN116, pp. 295–296.
126. SN133, pp.312–313.
127. SN128, p. 307.
128. SN129, p. 309.
129. SN130, pp. 309–310.
130. Ibid., p. 310.
131. SN135, pp. 314–315.
132. SN136, pp. 315–316.
133. SN137, pp. 316–317.
134. SN141, p. 325.
135. Ibid., pp. 325–326.
136. SN142, pp. 329–330.
137. SN144, pp. 331–332.
138. SN146, p. 334.

139. SN148, p. 336.
140. SN151, p. 339.
141. Ned Rorem, *Knowing When to Stop: A Memoir* (New York: Simon and Schuster, 1994), p. 509.
142. SN159, pp. 346–347.
143. SN160, pp. 347–348.
144. SN166, pp. 362–363.

PART TWO

1. SN23, p. 98. I did not directly ask Cardinal Mayer whether Nazarena wrote to him or the other priests after December 15, 1947, but there were none among those he gave me that could be dated any later. It seems certain that she chose to terminate her ministry as his "spiritual counselor" on the occasion of her profession.
2. SN24, pp. 101–102.
3. SN25, p. 109.
4. SN27, p. 112.
5. Ibid., pp. 113–114.
6. SN28, p. 115.
7. SN30, pp. 121–122.
8. Ibid., p. 123.
9. Ibid., pp. 124–125.
10. Ibid., p. 135.
11. Ibid., pp. 139–140.
12. SN31, p. 141.
13. Ibid., p. 142 *et passim.*
14. SN38, p. 171.
15. SN31, p. 143.
16. Ibid., pp. 143–144.
17. Ibid., pp. 144–145.
18. Ibid., p. 145.
19. SN32, p. 156.
20. Ibid., pp. 157–158.

21. Ibid., p. 153.
22. Ibid., p. 155.
23. Ibid., p. 154.
24. SN37, pp. 167–168.
25. SN34, p. 161.
26. Ibid., p. 162.
27. Ibid., pp. 163–164.
28. SN64, pp. 221–222.
29. Ibid., p. 221.
30. SN65, p. 223.
31. Ibid., p. 224.
32. SN93, p. 255.
33. Ibid.
34. SN94, pp. 256–257.
35. SN168, pp. 375–376.
36. SN107, pp. 278–279.
37. SN108, p. 280.
38. SN112, p. 285.
39. SN115, p. 293.
40. Ibid., pp. 280–281.
41. Ibid., p. 294.
42. SN112, p. 287.
43. cf. SN109, p. 281.
44. Ibid., pp. 281–282.
45. SN110, pp. 282–284.
46. SN111, p. 284.
47. SN112. pp. 285–290; all the references on the following pages are taken from this letter.
48. Ibid.; cf. Thomas Matus, *The Mystery of Romuald and the Five Brothers: Stories from the Benedictines and Camaldolese* (Big Sur, CA: Hermitage Books, 1995), p. 96 *et passim.*
49. Cf. St. John of the Cross, *Ascent of Mount Carmel* (2,7,5)
50. SN114, pp. 291–292.
51. SN115, pp. 293–295.

PART THREE

1. SN139, p. 322.

2. Ann K. Warren, "The Nun as Anchoress: England 1100–1500," in John A. Nichols and Lillian Thomas Shank, eds., *Distant Echoes, Medieval Religious Women*, Vol. 1, Cistercian Studies Series Number 71 (Kalamazoo: Cistercian Publications, 1984), pp. 197 and 199.

3. See note 49, part two.

4. J. Leclercq, F. Vandenbroucke, and L. Bouyer, *The Spirituality of the Middle Ages, A History of Christian Spirituality*, Vol. 2 (London: Burns & Oates, 1968), p. 12.

5. Thomas Merton, *Raids on the Unspeakable* (New York: New Directions, 1967), pp. 32–33.

6. "Best things dwell out of sight," in *The Complete Poems of Emily Dickinson*, edited by Thomas H. Johnson (Boston: Little, Brown & Co., 1960), p. 463.

7. SN161, pp. 348–357.

8. Nazarena is quoting an unknown author.

9. Cf. *Veni sancte Spiritus*, the sequence for the liturgy of Pentecost.

10. See note 49, part two.